W9-BVK-721

SAMS
Teach Yourself

Excel 97

by Jennifer Fulton

in 10 Minutes

SAMS

A Division of Macmillan Computer Publishing
201 West 103rd St., Indianapolis, Indiana 46290 USA

To Grandmother Ira Fulton. Thank you for your kindness, your love, and most of all, your grandson.

©1998 by Sams Publishing

All rights reserved. No part of this book shall be reproduced, stored in a retrieval system, or transmitted by any means, electronic, mechanical, photocopying, recording, or otherwise, without written permission from the publisher. No patent liability is assumed with respect to the use of the information contained herein. Although every precaution has been taken in the preparation of this book, the publisher and author assume no responsibility for errors or omissions. Neither is any liability assumed for damages resulting from the use of the information contained herein. For information, address Macmillan Publishing, 201 West 103rd Street, Indianapolis, Indiana 46290.

International Standard Book Number: 0-672-31326-x

Library of Congress Catalog Card Number: 98-84595

98 97   8 7 6 5 4 3 2 1

Interpretation of the printing code: the rightmost number of the first series of numbers is the year of the book's printing; the rightmost number of the second series of numbers is the number of the book's printing. For example, a printing code of 98-1 shows that the first printing of the book occurred in 1998.

Screen reproductions in this book were created using Collage Plus from Inner Media, Inc., Hollis, NH.

Printed in the United States of America

Publisher John Pierce

Managing Editor Thomas F. Hayes

Technical Editor Rick Brown

Production Editor Audra Gable

Book Designer Barbara Kordesh

Cover Designer Dan Armstrong

Production Team Angela Calvert, Cynthia Fields, Tricia Flodder, Janelle Herber, Pamela Woolf

Indexer Rebecca Hornyak

WE'D LIKE TO HEAR FROM YOU!

As part of our continuing effort to produce books of the highest possible quality, Sams would like to hear your comments. To stay competitive, we *really* want you, as a computer book reader and user, to let us know what you like or dislike most about this book or other Sams products.

You can mail comments, ideas, or suggestions for improving future editions to the address below, or send us a fax at (317) 581-4663. For the online-inclined, Macmillan Computer Publishing has a forum on CompuServe (type **GO QUEBOOKS** at any prompt) through which our staff and authors are available for questions and comments. The address of our Internet site is **http://www.mcp.com** (World Wide Web).

In addition to exploring our forum, please feel free to contact me personally to discuss your opinions of this book: I'm **75703,3251** on CompuServe, and I'm **lgentry@.mcp.com** on the Internet.

Although we cannot provide general technical support, we're happy to help you resolve problems you enounter related to our books, disks, or other products. If you need such assistance, please contact our Tech Support department at 800-545-5914 ext. 3833.

To order other Sams or Macmillan Computer publishing books or products, please call our customer service department at 800-835-3202 ext. 666.

Thanks in advance—your comments will help us to continue publishing the best books available on computer topics in today's market.

Lorna Gentry
Product Development Specialist
201 West 103rd Street
Indianapolis, Indiana 46290
USA

Contents

INTRODUCTION

Suppose you walked into work this morning and found Excel 97 sitting on your desk. On the box was a note from your supervisor that said "We need a budget report for Friday's meeting. See what you can do."

WHAT CAN YOU DO?

Well, you could start by wading through Excel's Help system to find out how to perform a specific task—but that might take a while, and you're running out of time. Anyway, the Help system might actually tell you more than you really want to know.

Because you're short on time (and patience), what you really need is a practical guide to Excel, one that tells you exactly how to create and print the worksheets, reports, and graphs you need for Friday's meeting.

WELCOME TO THE *SAMS' TEACH YOURSELF EXCEL 97 IN 10 MINUTES*

Because most people don't have the luxury of sitting down uninterrupted for hours at a time to learn Excel, this 10 Minute Guide does not attempt to teach everything about the program in huge chapters you don't have time to read. Instead, it focuses on the most often-used features, covering them in self-contained lessons designed to take 10 minutes or less to complete.

In addition, this 10 minute guide teaches you how to use Excel without relying on technical jargon. By providing straightforward, easy-to-follow explanations and lists of numbered steps that tell you which keys to press and which options to select, the *Sams' Teach Yourself Excel 97 in 10 Minutes* makes learning the program quick and easy.

Who Should Use the *Sams' Teach Yourself Excel 97 in 10 Minutes*?

The *Sams' Teach Yourself Excel 97 in 10 Minutes* is for anyone who:

- Needs to learn Excel quickly
- Feels overwhelmed or intimidated by the complexity of Excel
- Wants to learn the tasks necessary to accomplish his or her particular goals
- Wants a clear, concise guide to the most important features of Excel 97

How to Use This Book

The *Sams' Teach Yourself Excel 97 in 10 Minutes* consists of a series of lessons that cover some basic, intermediate, and advanced features. If this is your first encounter with Excel 97, you should probably work through Lessons 1 through 11 in order. Those lessons lead you through the process of creating, editing, and printing a spreadsheet. Subsequent lessons tell you how to use the more advanced features to customize your spreadsheet, including how to use your spreadsheet as a database; how to add, create, and print graphs (charts); and how to publish your work on the Internet.

If Excel 97 has not been installed on your computer, see the upcoming section "Installing Excel 97" for instructions on how to install the program.

Icons and Conventions Used in This Book

The following boxed sidebars have been scattered throughout the book to help you find your way around:

Timesaver Tip icons mark shortcuts and hints for using Excel efficiently.

 Plain English icons draw your attention to definitions of new terms.

 Panic Button icons denote places where new users often run into trouble.

 Upgrade Tip   These boxes help you identify features that are new to Excel 97 so you can quickly learn to take advantage of the advanced timesaving features of the latest version of Excel. In addition, you'll see some special tips along the way that identify how you can use Excel on the Internet.

In addition, the following conventions have been used to clarify the steps you must perform:

On-screen text	Any text that appears on-screen is shown in bold.
What you type	The information you type appears in bold and in color.
Menu names	The names of menus, commands, buttons, and dialog boxes are shown with the first letter capitalized for easy recognition.
Key+Key Combinations	In many cases, you must press a two-key combination to enter a command. For example, "Press Alt+X." In such cases, hold down the first key and press the second key.

INSTALLING EXCEL 97

Whether you have Microsoft Office 97 or Excel 97, these steps walk you through installing Excel on your computer's hard disk:

1. Insert Excel disk 1 in the floppy drive, or if you have an Excel CD, insert the CD in the CD-ROM drive. If you use the Excel CD, you won't have to insert any of the Excel disks during installation; you work with the CD only.

2. If you're using the Office CD, skip to step 3. If not, open the Start menu and choose Run to display the Run dialog box. In the Command Line text box, type **a:\setup** (for installation from a floppy) or **d:\setup** (for installation from a CD) and press Enter.

3. Click the Install Microsoft Office icon. Read the copyright message and click Continue.

4. Enter your Name and Organization and click OK. Click OK again to confirm the information.

5. When the Product ID is displayed, click OK.

6. (Optional) You can change the directory to which Excel is installed, but that's not really necessary. However, you might want to change to a different drive if the current drive does not have enough available disk space.

7. When prompted, select the Typical installation. This installs all of the essential Excel features.

8. Select the options you want installed and click Continue.

9. If Setup finds a previous version of Microsoft Office, it displays a message asking if you want it removed. Click Yes.

10. When the installation is complete, you'll see a message. Click OK. (If you have a modem, you can click Online Registration instead, to register you copy of Excel.)

Acknowledgments

Many thanks to the people at Sams who have helped me with this project. First, thanks to Martha O'Sullivan, Acquisitions Editor, for assigning this book to me. Thanks to Faithe Wempen, Product Development Specialist, for her help on developing this book. Thanks to Audra Gable, Production Editor, for keeping the manuscript in great shape. And thanks to all the other people at Sams who helped turn this book around on such an aggressive schedule.

Trademarks

All terms mentioned in this book that are known to be trademarks or service marks are listed below. In addition, terms suspected of being trademarks or service marks have been appropriately capitalized. Sams cannot attest to the accuracy of this information. Use of a term in this book should not be regarded as affecting the validity of any trademark or service mark.

Windows 95, Excel, and Toolbar are trademarks of Microsoft Corporation.

Starting and Exiting Excel

In this lesson, you'll learn how to start and end a typical Excel work session.

Starting Excel

After you installed Excel (as covered in the introduction of this book), the installation program returned you to the desktop. To start Excel from there, follow these steps:

1. Click the Start button, and the Start menu appears.

2. Choose Programs, and the Programs menu appears.

3. Choose the Microsoft Excel program item to start the program.

The Excel opening screen appears (see Figure 1.1), displaying a blank *workbook* labeled Book1. Excel is now ready for you to begin creating your workbook.

Workbook An Excel file is called a *workbook*. Each workbook consists of three worksheets (although you can add or remove worksheets as needed). Each worksheet consists of columns and rows that intersect to form boxes called *cells* into which you enter text. The tabs at the bottom of the workbook (labeled Sheet1, Sheet2, and so on) let you flip through the worksheets by clicking them with the mouse.

What's the Office Assistant? When you first start Excel, you're greeted by an animated icon called the Office Assistant. He's there to offer help, and he'll pop up from time to time whenever you encounter new features. You'll learn how to use the Office Assistant in Lesson 4. For now, close the Assistant by clicking Start Using Microsoft Excel.

If you installed the Office Shortcut Bar, you can also start Excel by clicking the Excel button on the Shortcut Bar. And finally, you can start Excel by opening an existing workbook. (You can do this only after you've created and saved a workbook, as you'll learn to do in upcoming lessons.) To start Excel and have Excel automatically open a workbook for you, follow these steps:

1. Click the Start button, and the Start menu appears.

2. Click Open Office Document. Excel displays the Open Office Document dialog box, displaying the contents of the My Documents folder.

3. Because you typically save your workbooks to the My Documents folder, they should be displayed at this point. However, if you don't see your workbook file listed, change to the folder that contains the workbook you want to open.

4. Click the workbook's file name to select it. Then click Open to open it and start Excel.

A LOOK AT THE EXCEL SCREEN

You will perform most operations in Excel using commands available through the menu bar at the top of the screen, and the Standard and Formatting toolbars just below the menu bar. In the next two lessons, you'll learn about the operations you can perform using the menu bar and the Standard toolbar.

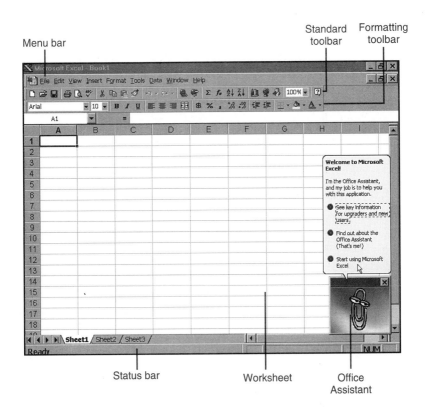

Menu bar

Standard toolbar

Formatting toolbar

Status bar

Worksheet

Office Assistant

FIGURE 1.1   Excel's opening screen displays a blank workbook named Book1.

EXITING EXCEL

To exit Excel and return to the Windows 95 desktop, perform either of these two steps:

- Open the File menu and select Exit.

  or

- Click the Close (X) button in the Excel window.

If you changed the workbook in any way without saving the file, Excel displays a prompt asking if you want to save the file before exiting. Select the desired option. See Lesson 7 for help in saving your workbook.

In this lesson, you learned how to start and exit Excel. In the next lesson, you'll learn about the Excel workbook window.

EXAMINING THE EXCEL WINDOW

In this lesson, you'll learn the basics of moving around in the Excel window and in the workbook window.

PARTS OF THE EXCEL WINDOW

As you can see in Figure 2.1, the Excel window contains many common Windows 95 elements, including a menu bar (from which you can select commands), a status bar (which displays the status of the current activity), and toolbars (which contain buttons and drop-down lists that provide quick access to common commands and features).

In addition, the window contains some elements that are unique to Excel, including:

Formula bar   When you enter information into a *cell*, anything you type appears in the Formula bar. The cell's location also appears in the Formula bar.

Cell   Each page in a workbook is a separate worksheet, and each worksheet contains a grid consisting of alphabetized columns and numbered rows. Where a row and column intersect, they form a box called a *cell*. Each cell has an *address* that consists of the column letter and row number (A1, B3, C4, and so on). You enter data and formulas in the cells to create your worksheets. You'll learn more about cells in Lessons 5 and 6.

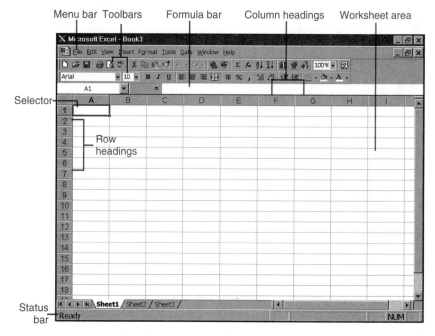

Menu bar Toolbars   Formula bar   Column headings   Worksheet area

Selector

Row headings

Status bar

FIGURE 2.1 Elements of the Excel workbook window.

Workbook window   Each Excel file is a workbook that consists of one or more worksheets. You can open several files (workbooks) at a time, each in its own window.

Column headings   The letters across the top of the worksheet, which identify the columns in the worksheet.

Row headings   The numbers down the side of the worksheet, which identify the rows in the worksheet.

Selector   The outline that indicates the active cell (the one in which you are working).

Missing Status Bar?   By default, Excel does not display its status bar. To display it, open the Tools menu, select Options, and click the View tab. In the Show area, select Status Bar and click OK.

MOVING FROM WORKSHEET TO WORKSHEET

By default, each workbook starts off with three worksheets. You can add worksheets to or delete worksheets from the workbook as needed. Because each workbook consists of one or more worksheets, you need a way of moving from worksheet to worksheet easily. Use one of the following methods:

- Press Ctrl+PgDn to move to the next worksheet or Ctrl+PgUp to move to a previous one.

  or

- Click the tab of the worksheet you want to go to (see Figure 2.2). If the tab is not shown, use the tab scroll buttons to bring the tab into view, and then click the tab.

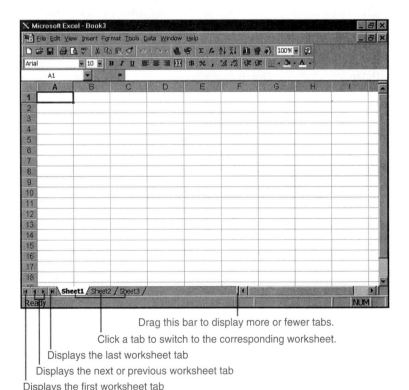

Drag this bar to display more or fewer tabs.
Click a tab to switch to the corresponding worksheet.
Displays the last worksheet tab
Displays the next or previous worksheet tab
Displays the first worksheet tab

FIGURE 2.2   You move from worksheet to worksheet with tabs.

MOVING WITHIN A WORKSHEET

Once the worksheet you want to work on is displayed, you'll need some way of moving to the various cells within the worksheet. Keep in mind that the part of the worksheet displayed on-screen is only a small piece of the actual worksheet. To move around the worksheet with your keyboard, use the keys listed in Table 2.1.

TABLE **2.1** MOVING AROUND A WORKSHEET WITH THE KEYBOARD

PRESS THIS	TO MOVE...
⇑ ⇓ ⇐ ⇒	One cell in the direction of the arrow.
Ctrl+⇑ or Ctrl+⇓	To the top or bottom of a data region (the area of a worksheet that contains data).
Ctrl+⇐ or Ctrl+⇒	To the leftmost or rightmost cell in a data region.
PgUp	Up one screen.
PgDn	Down one screen.
Home	Leftmost cell in a row.
Ctrl+Home	Upper-left corner of a worksheet.
Ctrl+End	Lower-right corner of the data area.
End+⇑, End+⇓, End+⇐, End+⇒	If the active cell is blank, moves in the direction of the arrow to the *first* cell that contains data. If the active cell contains an entry, moves in the direction of the arrow to the *last* cell that has an entry.

If you have a mouse, you can use the scroll bars to scroll to the area of the screen that contains the cell you want to work with. Then click the cell to make it the active cell.

Keep in mind that as you scroll, the scroll box moves within the scroll bar to tell you where you are within the file. In addition, the size of the scroll box changes to represent the amount of the total worksheet that is currently visible. If the scroll box is large, you know you're seeing most of the current worksheet in the window. If the scroll box is small, most of the worksheet is currently hidden from view.

Fast Scrolling   If you want to scroll to a specific row within a large worksheet, press and hold the Shift key while you drag the scroll box. The current row is displayed as you move the scroll box.

Move to a Specific Cell   To move quickly to a specific cell on a worksheet, type the cell's address in the Name box at the left end of the Formula bar and press Enter. A cell address consists of the column letter and row number that define the location of the cell (for example C25). To go to a cell on a specific worksheet, type the worksheet's name, an exclamation point, and the cell address (such as sheet3!C25) and press Enter.

SCROLLING THROUGH A WORKSHEET WITH THE INTELLIMOUSE

If you've installed the new Microsoft IntelliMouse (introduced with Excel 97), you can use it to move through a worksheet even more quickly than you can with a conventional mouse. Here's how:

To...	Do This...
Scroll a few rows	Rotate the wheel in the middle of the mouse forward or back.
Scroll faster (pan)	Click and hold the wheel button, and then drag the mouse in the direction in which you want to pan (scroll quickly). The further away from the origin mark (the four-headed arrow) you drag the mouse, the faster the panning action. To slow the pan, drag the mouse back towards the origin mark.

continues

To...	Do This...
Pan without holding	To pan without holding the wheel button down, simply click once, and then move the mouse in the direction in which you want to pan. You'll continue to pan when you move the mouse until you turn panning off by clicking the wheel again.

CHANGING THE VIEW OF YOUR WORKSHEET

There are many ways to change how your worksheet appears within the Excel window. Changing the view has no effect on how your worksheets will look when printed, but changing the view and getting a different perspective often helps you see your data more clearly. For example, you can enlarge or reduce the size of its text in order to view more or less of the worksheet at one time. You can also "freeze" row or column headings so you won't lose your place as you scroll through a large worksheet.

MAGNIFYING AND REDUCING THE WORKSHEET VIEW

| 100% ▼ | To enlarge or reduce your view of the current worksheet, use the Zoom feature. Simply click the |

Zoom button (on the Standard toolbar) and select the zoom percentage you want to use, such as 25% or 200%. You can enlarge a specific area of the worksheet if you'd like by selecting it first, opening the Zoom menu, and choosing Selection.

Fast Zoom   If you use the IntelliMouse, you can zoom in and out quickly by pressing and holding the Ctrl key as you move the wheel forward or back.

You can also display your worksheet so that it takes up the full screen—eliminating toolbars, Formula bar, status bar, and so on—as shown in Figure 2.3. To do so, open the View menu and select Full Screen. To return to normal view, click Close Full Screen.

Click here to exit full screen view.

FIGURE 2.3   View your worksheet in a full window.

FREEZING COLUMN AND ROW HEADINGS

As you scroll through a large worksheet, it's often helpful to freeze your headings so that you can view them with related data. For example, as you can see in Figure 2.4, you need to be able to view the column and row headings in order to understand the data in the cells.

Frozen column   With the headings frozen, you can scroll to view other months.

	A	H	I	J	K	L	M
1							
2							
3							
4		erprises					
5		enue					
6		o 78902					
7							
8							
9		July	August	September	October	November	Decembe
10	Mr. Mac	$ 6,521	$ 4,521	$ 2,000	$ -	$ -	$ -
11	Land Designer	$ 21,654	$ 22,548	$ 20,987	$ 25,497	$ 18,974	$ 21,9
12	Time Master	$ 10,556	$ 9,874	$ 10,255	$ 9,965	$ 11,254	$ 12,3
13	Tax 1996	$ -	$ -	$ -	$ -	$ -	$ -
14	Office Master	$ 25,497	$ 18,974	$ 21,954	$ 29,452	$ 25,487	$ 23,4
15	Personal Organizer	$ 9,965	$ 11,254	$ 12,354	$ 15,487	$ 12,541	$ 10,1
16	Home Designer	$ -	$ -	$ -	$ 12,315	$ 10,121	$ 9,8
17	Clean It!	$ 10,254	$ 9,987	$ 8,974	$ 10,556	$ 9,987	$ 9,8

FIGURE 2.4   As you scroll, the frozen headings remain in place.

To freeze row or column headings (or both), follow these steps:

1. Click the cell to the right of the row headings and/or below any column headings you want to freeze. This highlights the cell.

2. Open the Window menu and select Freeze Panes.

Play around a little, moving the cursor all around the document. As you do, the row and/or column headings remain locked in their positions. This enables you to view data in other parts of the worksheet without losing track of what that data represents. To unlock headings, open the Window menu again and select Unfreeze Panes.

SPLITTING WORKSHEETS

Sometimes when you're working with a large worksheet, you find
yourself wanting to view two parts of it at one time in order to
compare data. To view two parts of a worksheet, you *split* it. Figure 2.5 shows a split worksheet.

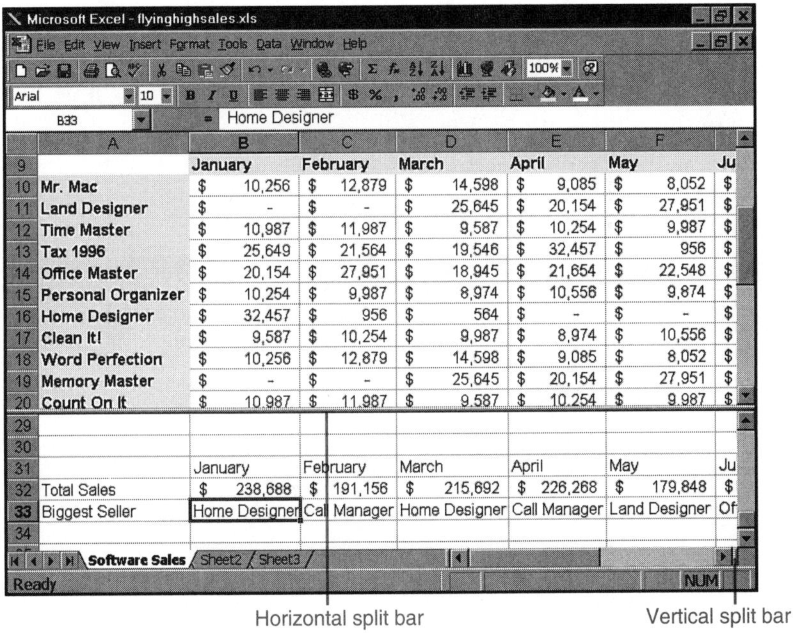

Horizontal split bar   Vertical split bar

FIGURE 2.5   Split a worksheet to view two parts at one time.

Follow these steps to split a worksheet:

1. Click either the vertical or the horizontal split bar.

2. Drag the split bar into the worksheet window.

3. Drop the split bar, and Excel splits the window at that
   location. When you scroll, the two panes automatically
   scroll in synch.

To remove the split, drag it back to its original position on the
scroll bar.

HIDING WORKBOOKS, WORKSHEETS, COLUMNS, AND ROWS

For those times when you're working on high priority or top secret information, you can hide workbooks, worksheets, columns or rows from prying eyes. For example, if you have confidential data stored in one particular worksheet, you can hide that worksheet, yet still be able to view the other worksheets in that workbook. You can also hide particular columns (see Figure 2.6) or rows within a worksheet—or even an entire workbook if you want.

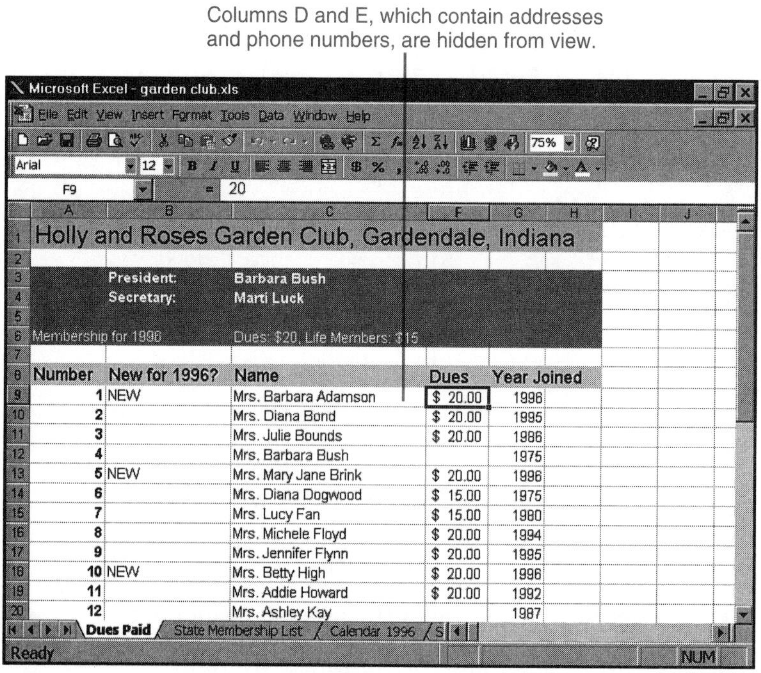

Columns D and E, which contain addresses and phone numbers, are hidden from view.

FIGURE 2.6   Hide data to prevent it from being viewed, printed, or changed.

In addition to hiding data in order to prevent it from appearing on a report, you might hide it to prevent it from accidentally being changed. When data is hidden, it cannot be viewed, printed, or changed. This is *unlike* other changes you might make to the view (such as changing the Zoom), which do not affect your worksheet when printed. Hiding data *does* prevent that data from being printed.

Use these methods to hide data:

- To hide a *workbook*, open the Window menu and select Hide.

- To hide a *worksheet*, click its tab to select it. Then open the Format menu, select Sheet, and select Hide.

- To hide *rows* or *columns*, click a row or column heading to select it. Then open the Format menu, select Row or Column, and select Hide.

Hide More Than One　　To select several worksheets, press and hold Ctrl while you click each tab. To select several rows or columns, press and hold Ctrl while you click each heading.

Of course, whenever you need to, you can easily redisplay the hidden data. To redisplay hidden data, select the hidden area first. For example, select the rows, columns, or sheets adjacent to the hidden ones. Then repeat the previous steps, selecting Unhide from the appropriate menus.

You Can't Hide It Completely!　　It's easy to undo the command to hide data, so you can't really hide data completely as a means of security. If you give the workbook file to someone else, for example, he or she can easily unhide and view the data you hid.

In this lesson, you learned about the elements of the Excel window and how to move around within workbooks and worksheets. You also learned how to change the view of your worksheet, freeze column and row headings, and hide data. In the next lesson, you will learn how to use Excel's toolbars.

USING EXCEL'S TOOLBARS

In this lesson, you will learn how to use Excel's toolbars to save time when you work. You will also learn how to arrange them for maximum performance.

USING THE TOOLBARS

Unless you tell it otherwise, Excel displays the Standard and Formatting toolbars as shown in Figure 3.1. To select a tool from a toolbar, simply click the tool.

 Off Duty If a tool appears grayed, it is currently unavailable. Tools become unavailable when they are not applicable to your current activity.

 What Is a Toolbar? An Excel toolbar is a collection of tools or icons displayed in a long bar that can be moved and reshaped to make it more convenient for you to use. Each icon represents a common command or task.

Here are some easy ways to learn about the available toolbar buttons:

- To view the name of a button, position the mouse pointer over it. Excel displays a ScreenTip, which displays the name of the button (as shown in Figure 3.1).

- To get help with the command associated with a particular button, press Shift+F1. The mouse pointer changes to a question mark. Move the question mark pointer over a button and click it.

Standard Formatting A grayed button is not When you point to a button, its
toolbar toolbar currently available. name appears in a ScreenTip.

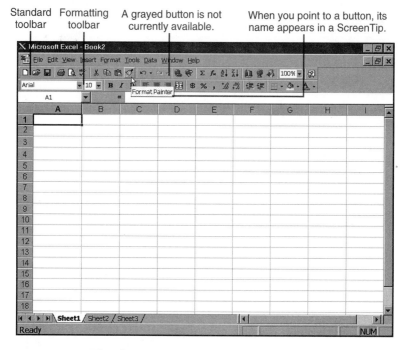

FIGURE 3.1 The Standard and Formatting toolbars contain buttons for Excel's most commonly used features.

TURNING TOOLBARS ON AND OFF

By default, Excel initially displays the Standard and Formatting toolbars. If you find that you don't use these toolbars, you can turn one or both of them off to free up some screen space. In addition, you can turn on other toolbars (although some toolbars appear on their *own* when you perform a related activity).

Follow these steps to turn a toolbar on or off:

1. Open the View menu and choose Toolbars. A submenu appears.

2. A check mark next to a toolbar's name indicates that the toolbar is currently being displayed. To turn a toolbar on or off (whichever it's not), simply click its name in the list to add or remove the check mark.

Quick View   To display a hidden toolbar quickly, right-click on an existing toolbar and select the toolbar you want to display from the shortcut menu.

Excel on the Web   Excel for Windows 97 allows you to open Web pages within its window, which you'll learn to do in Lesson 21. When you're working on the Web, the Web toolbar is displayed. Because the other Excel toolbars are unnecessary in such a situation, you can quickly remove them from the screen by clicking the Show Only Web Toolbar button.

Moving Toolbars

After you have displayed the toolbars you need, you can position them in your work area where they are most convenient. Figure 3.2 shows an Excel screen with three toolbars in various positions on the screen.

Here's what you do to move a toolbar:

1. Click a toolbar's move handle. (If the toolbar is floating in the middle of the window, click its title bar instead.)

2. Hold down the mouse button and drag the toolbar to where you want it. You can drag it to a side of the window (to a "dock") or let it "float" anywhere in the window.

Although you can drag a toolbar anywhere, if you drag one that contains a drop-down list (such as the Standard or Formatting toolbars) to the left or right side of the window, the drop-down list buttons disappear. If you move the toolbar back to the top or bottom of the window (or let it float) the drop-down list buttons reappear.

Move
handle

Floating
toolbar

Formatting toolbar
was left at the top.

Standard toolbar has
been moved to the bottom.

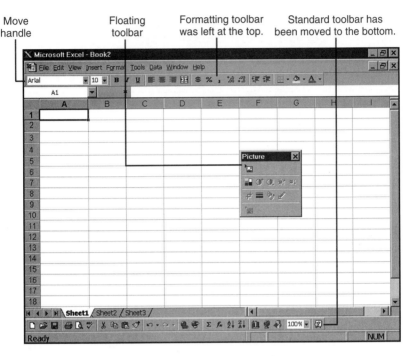

FIGURE 3.2   Three toolbars in various positions.

    Floating Toolbar   A floating toolbar acts just like a window. You can drag its title bar to move it or drag a border to size it. If you drag a floating toolbar to the top or bottom of the screen, it turns back into a horizontal toolbar.

    Quickly Moving a Toolbar   To quickly move a floating toolbar to the top of the screen, double-click its title bar. To move a docked toolbar into the middle of the window, double-click its move handle.

In Excel for Windows 97, the worksheet menu bar is treated the same as other toolbars. This means you can move it to the side of a window, or you can float it in the middle if you want. It also means that you can customize the menu bar in a manner similar to toolbars, as discussed in the next section.

Customizing the Toolbars

If Excel's toolbars provide too few (or too many) options for you, you can create your own toolbars or customize existing toolbars. To customize a toolbar, follow these steps:

1. Right-click on any toolbar and choose Customize from the shortcut menu, or open the Tools menu and select Customize.

2. If the toolbar you want to customize is not currently visible, click the Toolbars tab and select it from the list. The toolbar appears.

3. To change the size of the toolbar icons, to turn on or off ScreenTips, or to change the animation of your menus, click the Options tab. On the Options tab, select the options you want to apply. For example, to make the toolbar icons larger, click the Large icons option.

4. To add or remove buttons from a toolbar, click the Commands tab.

5. To add a button to a toolbar, select its category. (For example, to add the Clear Contents button to a toolbar, select the Edit category.) You can add menus to a toolbar as well; you'll find them listed at the bottom of the Categories list. Once you've selected the proper category, click the command you want and drag it onto the toolbar, as shown in Figure 3.3.

Drag a button to a bar to add it.

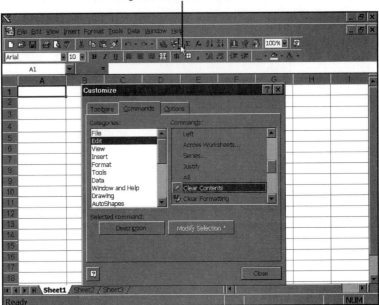

FIGURE 3.3   To add a button to a toolbar, drag it there.

Don't Know What an Option Is For?   Simply select the command and then click Description to learn what that command does.

6. To remove a button from a toolbar, drag it off the toolbar.

7. To rearrange the buttons on a toolbar, drag them around within the bar.

8. Click the Close button when you're done.

If you mess up a toolbar, you can return to its default settings (the way it was before you or someone else changed it). From within the Customize dialog box, click Toolbars, highlight the name of the toolbar you want to reset, and then click the Reset button.

CREATING YOUR OWN TOOLBAR

Instead of changing any of the standard Excel toolbars, you can create one of your own and fill it with the tools you use most often. Follow these steps to learn how:

1. Open the Tools menu and select Customize.

2. Click the Toolbars tab.

3. Click the New button.

4. Type a name for your new toolbar (such as Jen's Favorites) and click OK. Excel creates a new floating toolbar.

5. Click the Commands tab, select the proper category for a desired button, and then drag it onto the toolbar.

6. Repeat step 5 to add more buttons to your new toolbar. When you finish, click Close.

If you want delete a custom toolbar, open the Tools menu and select Customize. In the Toolbars list, click the custom toolbar you want to delete. Then click the Delete button in the Customize dialog box.

In this lesson, you learned how to use Excel's toolbars and to customize them for your own unique needs. In the next lesson, you'll learn how to enter different types of data.

4 LESSON GETTING HELP

In this lesson, you'll learn about the various types of help available to you in Excel.

WHAT KIND OF HELP IS AVAILABLE?

Because every person is different, Excel offers many different ways to get help with the program. You can:

- Ask the Office Assistant for help.

- Get help on a particular element you see on-screen with the What's This? tool.

- Choose what you're interested in learning about from a series of Help Topics.

- If you have a connection to the Internet, you can access the Microsoft On the Web feature to view Web pages containing help information.

ASKING THE OFFICE ASSISTANT FOR HELP

You have probably already met the Office Assistant: it's the paper clip character that popped up to give you advice when you started Excel the first time. Don't let its whimsical appearance fool you, though. Behind the Office Assistant is a very powerful Help system.

Upgrade Tip   The Office Assistant replaces the Answer Wizard feature from Excel for Windows 95.

TURNING THE OFFICE ASSISTANT ON OR OFF

When you started Excel for the first time, Office Assistant appeared, offering its help. The Office Assistant sits in a little box on top of whatever you're working on, as shown in Figure 4.1. You can leave Office Assistant on-screen even when you're not using it. However, if it gets in the way, you can turn it off by clicking the Close (X) button in its upper-right corner.

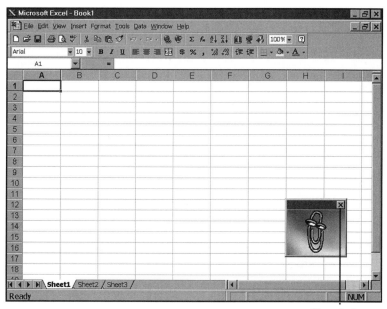

Close button

FIGURE 4.1   The Office Assistant appears in its own window.

   To turn the Office Assistant on again, click the Office Assistant button on the Standard toolbar or press F1.

 Always There   When you turn on the Office Assistant in Excel, he appears in your other Office programs as well. Likewise, if you close the Office Assistant while in Excel, he also disappears from your other Office program windows.

KINDS OF HELP

When you first turn on the Office Assistant, a bubble appears next to (or above) its box asking you what kind of help you want (see Figure 4.2). You can do any of the following:

- Type a question in the text box to tell the Office Assistant what kind of help you need. (More on this shortly.)

- Select one of the Office Assistant's "guesses" about what you need help with.

- Click the Tips button to get any tips the Office Assistant can provide for the task you're currently performing.

- Click the Options button to customize the way the Office Assistant works.

- Click Close to close the bubble (but leave the Office Assistant on-screen).

If you leave Office Assistant on-screen but close the help bubble, you can make the bubble reappear by clicking the Office Assistant's title bar.

 May I Make a Suggestion? Sometimes you'll see a light bulb next to the Office Assistant in its window, or on the Office Assistant button on the Standard toolbar. The light bulb means that the Office Assistant has a suggestion for you regarding the task you're currently performing. To view the suggestion, click the light bulb in the Office Assistant window. When you finish reading the suggestion, click the Close button.

ASKING THE OFFICE ASSISTANT A QUESTION

If you need help on a particular topic, you type a question into the text box (refer to Figure 4.2). Follow these steps to see Office Assistant in action:

1. If the Office Assistant is not visible, click the Office Assistant button on the Standard toolbar. If the Assistant is

visible but the help bubble is not, click the Office
Assistant's title bar.

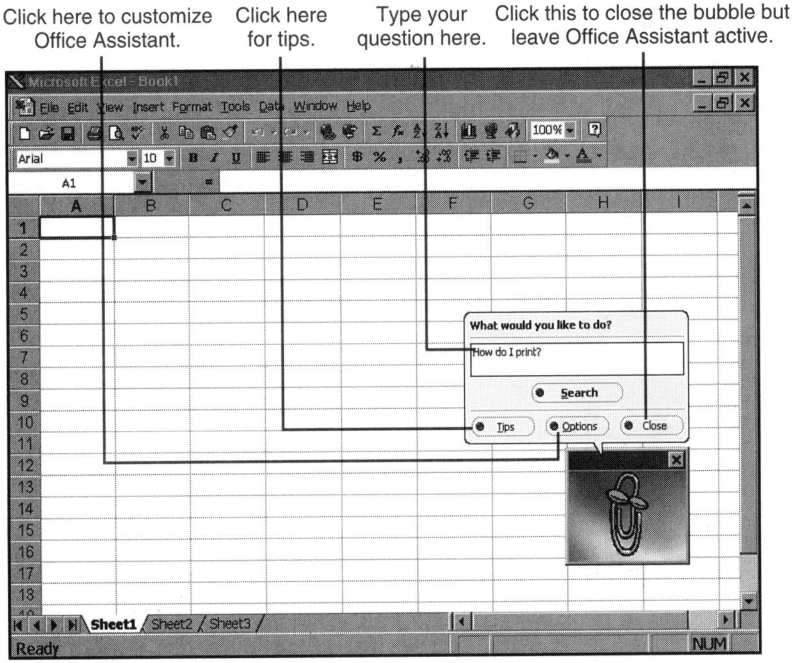

Click here to customize   Click here   Type your   Click this to close the bubble but
Office Assistant.   for tips.   question here. leave Office Assistant active.

FIGURE 4.2   Office Assistant is at your service.

2. Type a question into the text box. For instance, you might
   type **How do I print?** to get help on printing your work.

3. Click the Search button or press Enter. Office Assistant
   displays some topics that might match what you're looking for. For instance, Figure 4.3 shows Office Assistant's
   answer to the question "How do I print?"

4. Click the option that best describes what you're trying
   to do. For instance, you might choose **What to do before you print** from Figure 4.3. A Help window appears with instructions for the specified task.

   If none of the options describe what you want, click the
   See More... arrow to view more options, or type a different
   question into the text box.

Click an option.

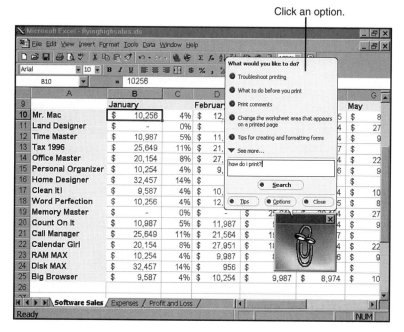

FIGURE 4.3 The Office Assistant asks you to narrow down exactly what you are trying to accomplish so it can provide the best help possible.

The Help window that appears containing the task instructions is part of the same Help system that you can access with the Help, Contents and Index command. See "Managing Help Topics You've Located" later in this lesson for information about navigating this window.

USING THE EXCEL HELP TOPICS

A more conventional way to get help is through the Contents and Index command on the Help menu. When you open the Excel Help system, you move through the topics listed to find the topic you're interested in.

There are several tabs in the Help system that enable you to use Help the way you want to. To access the Help system, follow these steps:

1. Open the Help menu and select Contents and Index.

2. Click the tab for the type of help you want (the tabs are explained in the next sections).

3. If there's a list of topics, click the topic you're interested in; if not, type your topic and press Enter.

The following sections contain information about each tab.

THE CONTENTS TAB

The Contents tab of the Help system is a series of "books" you can open. Each book has one or more Help topics in it, and some books contain other subbooks! Figure 4.4 shows a Contents screen.

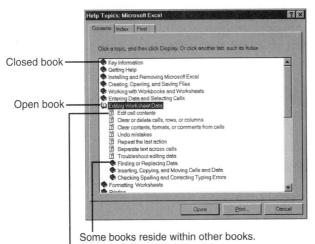

FIGURE 4.4 The Help Contents screen.

To select a Help topic from the Contents screen, follow these steps:

1. Open the Help menu and select Contents and Index.

2. Click the Contents tab.

3. Find the book that describes, in broad terms, what you're looking for help with. Double-click the book, and a list of Help topics appears below the book (see Figure 4.4).

4. Double-click a Help topic to display it.

5. When you finish reading a topic, click Help Topics to go back to the main Help screen, or click the window's Close (X) button to exit Help.

THE INDEX TAB

The Index is an alphabetical listing of every Help topic available. It's like an index in a book. Follow these steps to use the Index:

1. Open the Help menu and select Contents and Index.

2. Click the Index tab.

3. Type the first few letters of the topic you're looking for, and the index list jumps quickly to that spot (see Figure 4.5).

4. Double-click the topic you want to see.

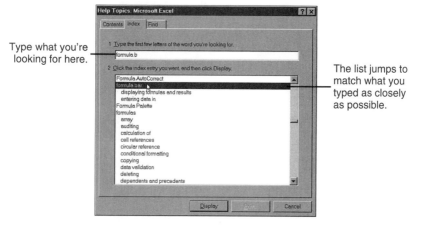

Type what you're looking for here.

The list jumps to match what you typed as closely as possible.

FIGURE 4.5   Browse through topics alphabetically in the Index.

THE FIND TAB

The Index is great if you know the name of the Help topic you're looking for. But what if you're not sure? That's where Find comes in handy. Find searches not only the titles of Help topics, but also their contents, and retrieves all the topics in which the word(s) you typed appears. Follow these steps to learn how to use Find:

1. Open the Help menu and select Help Topics and Index.

2. Click the Find tab. The first time you use Find, you'll be asked to build the Find index. Click Next to do so, and then click Finish.

3. Type the topic you're looking for in the top box, as shown in Figure 4.6.

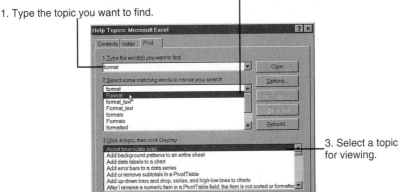

2. Click the word that most closely matches what you want.

1. Type the topic you want to find.

3. Select a topic for viewing.

FIGURE 4.6 Use Find to locate all the Help topics that deal with a certain subject.

4. If more than one line appears in the middle box, click the one that most closely matches your interest.

5. Browse the topics that appear at the bottom, and double-click the one that describes the help you need. A Help window for the topic you selected appears.

MANAGING HELP TOPICS YOU'VE LOCATED

No matter which of the four avenues you choose for finding a Help topic (the Office Assistant, Contents, Index, or Find), you eventually end up at a Help screen of instructions like the one shown in Figure 4.7. When you do, you can read the information on-screen or do any of the following:

- Click any underlined word (such as the word "formula" in Figure 4.7) to see a definition of it.

- Click the Show Me button (when it's available) to have Excel walk you through the steps for a procedure.

- Click a button to jump to another Help screen. For instance, in Figure 4.7, the >> buttons at the top and bottom of the Help window take you to screens of related information when you click them.

- Print a hard copy of the information by clicking the Options button and selecting Print Topic.

- Copy the text to the Clipboard (for pasting into a program such as Microsoft Word or Windows Notepad) by clicking the Options button and selecting Copy.

- Return to the previous Help topic you viewed by clicking the Back button.

- Return to the main Help Topics screen by clicking the Help Topics button.

- Close the Help window by clicking the Close (X) button.

Excel on the Web   New for Excel 97 is built-in access to Microsoft's Web site, where you can find additional Help information. To view it, establish your Internet connection and start your Web browser. Then open the Help menu, select Microsoft on the Web, and choose from the Web pages listed on the submenu to jump directly to one of them.

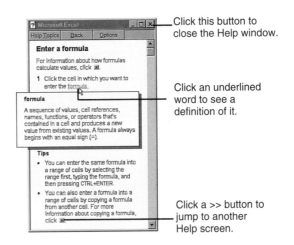

Click this button to close the Help window.

Click an underlined word to see a definition of it.

Click a >> button to jump to another Help screen.

FIGURE 4.7 Once you arrive at the information you need, you can read it on-screen, print it, or move to another Help topic.

GETTING HELP WITH SCREEN ELEMENTS

If you wonder about the function of a particular button or tool on the screen, wonder no more. Just follow these steps to find out what it does:

1. Press Shift+F1, or open the Help menu and select What's This? The mouse pointer changes to a question mark.

2. With the question mark pointer, click on the screen element for which you want help. A box appears explaining the element.

If you need help with an element in a dialog box, click the Help button at the end of the title bar. (It looks like a big question mark.) Point to an element and click, and you'll get instant help.

In this lesson, you learned about the many forms of help that Excel offers. In the next lesson, you'll learn to enter various types of data into your Excel worksheet.

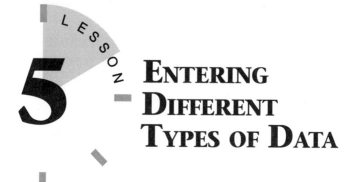

5 LESSON
ENTERING DIFFERENT TYPES OF DATA

In this lesson, you will learn how to enter different types of data in an Excel worksheet.

THE DATA TYPES

To create a worksheet that does something, you must enter data into the cells that make up the worksheet. There are many types of data that you ca9n enter, including:

- Text
- Numbers
- Dates
- Times
- Formulas
- Functions

In this lesson, you'll learn how to enter text, numbers, dates, and times. In Lessons 14, 15, and 16, you'll learn how to enter formulas and functions.

ENTERING TEXT

Text is any combination of letters, numbers, and spaces. By default, text is automatically left-aligned in a cell.

To enter text into a cell:

1. Click in the cell in which you want to enter text.

2. Type the text. As you type, your text appears in the cell and in the Formula bar, as shown in Figure 5.1.

3. Press Enter. Your text appears in the cell, left-aligned. (You can also press Tab or an arrow key to enter the text and move to another cell.) If you've made a mistake and you want to abandon your entry, press Esc instead.

Row headings   Column headings

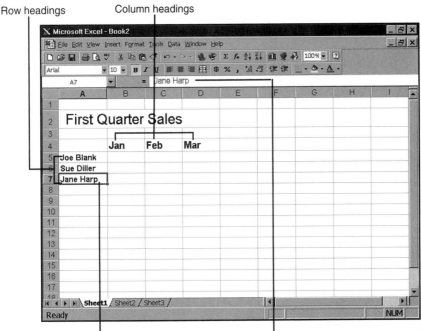

As you enter text into a cell...   ...it appears in the Formula bar.

FIGURE 5.1 Data that you enter also appears in the Formula bar as you type it.

But It Doesn't Fit!   To widen a column to display all of its data, move to the column headings bar at the top of the worksheet. Then double-click the *right* border of the column you want to "autofit" to hold your data. See Lesson 20 for more help.

Numbers As Text   You might want to enter a number that will be treated as text (such as a ZIP code). To do so, precede the entry with a single quotation mark ('), as in '46220. The single quotation mark is an alignment prefix that tells Excel to treat the following characters as text and left-align them in the cell.

ENTERING COLUMN AND ROW HEADINGS

Column and row headings identify your data. Column headings appear across the top of the worksheet beneath the title. Row headings are entered on the left side of the worksheet, usually in Column A.

Column headings describe what the numbers in a column represent. Typically, column headings specify time periods such as years, months, days, dates, and so on. Row headings describe what the numbers in each row represent. Typically, row headings specify data categories, such as product names, employee names, or income and expense items in a budget.

When entering column headings, press the Tab key to move from one cell to the next instead of pressing Enter. When entering row headings, use the down arrow key instead.

Entering Similar Data As Headings   When you need to enter similar data (such as a series of months or years) as column or row headings, there's a trick for entering them quickly. See the section, "Entering a Series with AutoFill," later in this lesson for help.

ADDING COMMENTS TO CELLS

You can use cell comments to provide detailed information about data in a worksheet. For example, you can create a comment to help remind you of the purpose behind a particular formula or data that should be updated. Once you create a comment, you

can display it at any time. To add a comment to a cell, do the
following:

1. Select the cell to which you want to add a comment.

2. Open the Insert menu and choose Comment or click the
   New Comment button on the Reviewing toolbar.

3. Type your comment, as shown in Figure 5.2.

4. Click outside the cell. A red triangle appears in the upper-
   right corner of the cell to show that it contains a comment.

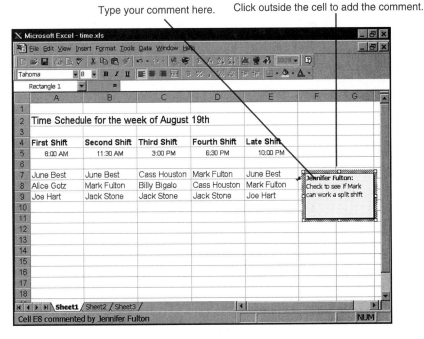

FIGURE 5.2   Adding a cell comment.

To view comments later, point to any cell that contains a red dot
in its upper right corner. Excel displays the comment.

To edit a comment, select the cell that contains the note and
choose Insert Edit, Comment. Make your changes, and then click
outside the cell to save them. To delete a comment, click the cell,
select Edit, Clear, and then select Comments.

ENTERING NUMBERS

Valid numbers can include the numeric characters 0–9 and any of these special characters: + – / . , ( ) $ %. This means that you can include commas, decimal points, dollar signs, percent signs, and parentheses in the values that you enter.

Although you can include punctuation when you type your entries, you may not want to. For example, instead of typing a column of dollar amounts including dollar signs, commas, and decimal points, you can type numbers such as 700 and 81295, and then format the column with currency formatting. Excel then changes your entries to $700.00 and $81,295.00 or to $700 and $81295, depending on the number of decimal points you specify. See Lesson 17 for more information.

To enter a number:

1. Click the cell into which you want to enter a number.

2. Type the number. To enter a negative number, precede it with a minus sign or surround it with parentheses. To enter a fraction, precede it with a 0, as in 0 1/2.

3. Press Enter, and the number appears in the cell, right-aligned.

 ####### If you enter a number and it appears in the cell as all pound signs (#######) or in scientific notation (such as 7.78E+06), don't worry—the number is okay. The cell just isn't wide enough to display the entire number. To fix it, move to the column headings at the top of the worksheet and double-click on the right border of the column. The column expands to fit the largest entry. See Lesson 20 for more help.

ENTERING DATES AND TIMES

You can enter dates and times in a variety of formats. When you enter a date using a format shown in Table 5.1, Excel converts the date into a number that reflects the number of days between

January 1, 1900 and that date. Even though you won't see this number (Excel displays your entry as a normal date), the number is used whenever you use this date in a calculation. By the way, the feature that automatically formats your data based on the way you enter it is called AutoFormat.

TABLE 5.1   VALID FORMATS FOR DATES AND TIMES

FORMAT	EXAMPLE
M/D	4/8
M-YY	4-58
MM/DD/YY	4/8/58 or 04/08/58
MMM—YY	Jan—92
MMMMMMMM-YY	September-93
MMMMMMMM DD, YYYY	September 3, 1993
DD—MMM—YY	28—Oct—91
DD—MMM	6—Sep
HH:MM	16:50
HH:MM:SS	8:22:59
HH:MM AM/PM	7:45 PM
HH:MM:SS AM/PM	11:45:16 AM
MM/DD/YY HH:MM	11/8/80 4:20

Follow these steps to learn how to enter a date or time:

1. Click the cell into which you want to enter a date or time.

2. Type the date or time in the format in which you want it displayed. You can use hyphens (-) or slashes (/).

3. Press Enter. As long as Excel recognizes the entry as a date or time, it appears right-aligned in the cell. If Excel doesn't recognize it, it's treated as text and left-aligned.

If you're entering a column of dates, you can specify the date format you want first. Then as you type your dates, Excel will automatically adapt them to fit that format. For example, suppose you like the MMMMMMMMM DD, YYYY format. Instead of typing each date in full, you could select that format for the column and then type 9/3/93, and Excel would change it to display September 3, 1993. To format a column, click the column header to select the column. Then open the Format menu and select Cells. On the Numbers tab, select the date format you want. (See Lesson 6 for more help.)

 Not Wide Enough? If you enter a long date and it appears in the cell as all number signs (#######), Excel is trying to tell you that the column is not wide enough to display it.

 Day or Night? Unless you type AM or PM after your time entry, Excel assumes that you are using a 24-hour military clock. Therefore, 8:20 is assumed to be AM, not PM. So if you mean PM, type the entry as 8:20 PM (or 8:20 p if you want to use a shortcut). Note that you must type a space between the time and the AM or PM notation.

COPYING ENTRIES QUICKLY

You can copy an existing entry into surrounding cells by performing the following steps:

1. Click the fill handle of the cell whose contents you want to copy.

2. Drag the fill handle down or to the right to copy the data to adjacent cells (see Figure 5.3). A bubble appears to let you know *exactly* what data is being copied.

Fill handle   The bubble lets you see what you're copying.

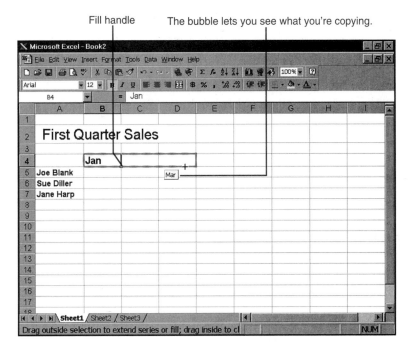

FIGURE 5.3   Drag the fill handle to copy the contents and formatting into neighboring cells.

If you're copying a number, a month, or other item that might be interpreted as a series (such as January, February, etc.), but you *don't* want to create a series—you just want to copy the contents of the cell exactly—press and hold Ctrl as you drag the fill handle.

Copying Across Worksheets   You can copy the contents of cells from one worksheet to one or more worksheets in the workbook. First select the worksheet(s) you want to copy to by clicking the sheet tabs while holding down the Ctrl key. Then select the cells you want to copy (see Lesson 6). Open the Edit menu, select Fill, and select Across Worksheets. Then select All (to copy both the cells' contents and their formatting), Contents, or Formats, and click OK.

ENTERING A SERIES WITH AUTOFILL

Entering a series (such as January, February, and March or 1994, 1995, 1996, and 1997) is similar to copying a cell's contents. As you drag the fill handle of the original cell, AutoFill does all the work for you, interpreting the first entry and creating a series of entries based on it. For example, if you type Monday in a cell, and then drag the cell's fill handle over some adjacent cells, you'll create the series Monday, Tuesday, Wednesday.... As you drag, the bubble lets you know exactly what you're copying so that you can stop at the appropriate cell to create exactly the series you want.

ENTERING A CUSTOM SERIES

Although AutoFill is good for a brief series of entries, you may encounter situations in which you need more control. Excel can handle several different types of series, as shown in Table 5.2.

TABLE 5.2   DATA SERIES

SERIES	INITIAL ENTRIES	RESULTING SERIES
Linear	1,2	1, 2, 3, 4
	100,99	100, 99, 98, 97
	1,3	1, 3, 5, 7
Growth	10, 20	10, 20, 30, 40
	10, 50	10, 50, 90, 130
Date	Mon, Wed	Mon, Wed, Fri
	Feb, May	Feb, May, Aug
	Qtr1, Qtr3	Qtr1, Qtr3, Qtr1
	1992, 1995	1992, 1995, 1998

Basically, you make two sample entries for your series in adjacent cells, and Excel uses them to calculate the rest of the series. Here's what you do:

1. Enter the first value in one cell and press Enter.

2. Move to the second cell and enter the next value in the series.

3. Select both cells by dragging over them. (See Lesson 6 for more information.) Excel highlights the cells.

4. Drag the fill handle over as many adjacent cells as necessary. Excel computes your series and fills the selected cells with the appropriate values, as shown in Figure 5.4.

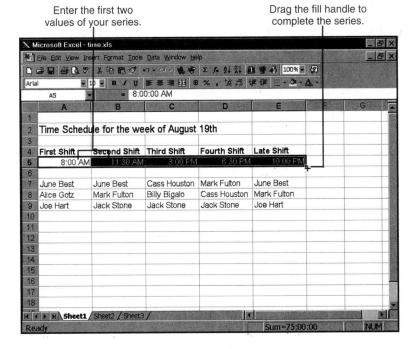

FIGURE 5.4 Drag to create your series.

ENTERING THE SAME DATA OVER AND OVER WITH AUTOCOMPLETE

When you type the first few letters of an entry, AutoComplete intelligently completes the entry for you based on the entries you've already made in that particular column. AutoComplete works with data entered in columns only, not rows. For example, suppose you want to enter the countries of origin for a series of packages. You type the name of a country once, and the next time you start to type that entry, AutoComplete inserts it for you.

By default, AutoComplete is always turned on, so you don't have to worry about that. However, if it drives you crazy, you can turn it off with the Tools, Options command. Click the Edit tab and click the Enable AutoComplete for Cell Values option to turn it off.

Follow these steps to try out AutoFormat:

1. Type **England** into a cell and press the down arrow key to move to the next cell down. Type **Spain** and press the down arrow key again. Then type **Italy** and press the down arrow key.

2. Type **e** again, and "England" appears in the cell. Press Enter to accept the entry. (Likewise, the next time you type **i** or **s**, "Italy" or "Spain" will appear.)

3. To see a list of AutoComplete entries, right-click a cell and select Pick From List from the shortcut menu. Excel shows you a PickList of entries (in alphabetical order) that it has automatically created from the words you've typed in the column.

4. Click a word in the PickList to insert it in the selected cell.

In this lesson, you learned how to enter different types of data and how to automate data entry. In the next lesson, you will learn how to edit entries.

EDITING ENTRIES

6

In this lesson, you will learn how to change data and how to undo those changes if necessary. You'll also learn how to copy, move, and delete data.

EDITING DATA

After you have entered data into a cell, you may edit it in either the Formula bar or in the cell itself.

To edit an entry in Excel:

1. Click the cell in which you want to edit data.

2. To begin editing, click the Formula bar, press F2, or double-click the cell. This puts you in Edit mode; the word **Edit** appears in the status bar.

3. Press ⇐ or ⇒ to move the insertion point within the entry. Press the Backspace key to delete characters to the left of the insertion point; press the Delete key to delete characters to the right. Then type any characters you want to add.

4. Click the Enter button on the Formula bar or press Enter on the keyboard to accept your changes.

Or, if you change your mind and you no longer want to edit your entry, click the Cancel button or press Esc.

CHECKING YOUR SPELLING

Excel offers a spell checking feature that rapidly finds and high-lights misspellings in a worksheet.

To run the spelling checker, follow these steps:

1. Click the Spelling button on the Standard toolbar. Excel finds the first misspelled word and displays it at the top of the Spelling dialog box. A suggested correction then appears in the Change To box (see Figure 6.1).

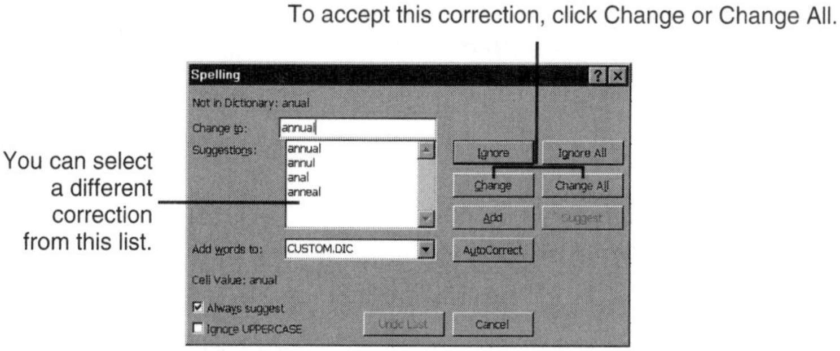

To accept this correction, click Change or Change All.

You can select
a different
correction
from this list.

Figure 6.1 Correct spelling mistakes with the options in the Spelling dialog box.

2. To accept the suggestion and change the misspelled word, click Change. Or, click Change All to change all occurrences of the misspelled word.

3. If the suggestion in the Change To box is not correct, you can do any of the following:

    *   Select a different suggestion from the Suggestions box, and then click Change or Change All. (You can display additional words in the Suggestions list by clicking Suggest.)

    *   Type your own correction in the Change To box, and then click Change or Change All.

    *   Click Ignore to leave the word unchanged.

    *   Click Ignore All to leave all occurrences of the word unchanged.

    *   Click Add to add the word to the dictionary so Excel won't ever flag it as misspelled again.

4. When the spelling checker can't find any more misspelled words, it displays a prompt telling you that the spelling check is complete. Click OK to confirm that the spelling check is finished.

 Choose the Wrong Option? If you mistakenly select the wrong option, you can click the Undo Last button in the Spelling dialog box to undo the last selection you made.

USING AUTOCORRECT TO CORRECT SPELLING MISTAKES

Excel's AutoCorrect feature automatically corrects common typing mistakes as you type. If you type a mistake (such as "teh" instead of "the") and press Enter, Excel enters the corrected text in the cell. AutoCorrect also corrects two initial capitals. For example, if you type "MAine" and press Enter, Excel will enter "Maine" in the cell. In addition, AutoCorrect capitalizes the first letter of a sentence and the names of days.

You can teach AutoCorrect the errors you normally make, and have it correct them for you as you type. For example, if you always type "breif" instead of "brief," you can add it to the AutoCorrect list. You can also use AutoCorrect to replace an abbreviation, such as ndiv, with the words it represents: Northern Division. Here's how:

1. Open the Tools menu and select AutoCorrect. The AutoCorrect dialog box appears.

2. Type your error in the Replace text box.

3. Type the correction in the With text box.

4. Click Add to add the entry to the AutoCorrect list.

5. If you want to delete an entry from the AutoCorrect list, select it from the list and click the Delete button.

Too Quick!   If you want to turn AutoCorrect off because it's "correcting" your entries before you get a chance to stop it, turn off the Replace Text As You Type option in the AutoCorrect dialog box.

UNDOING AN ACTION

You can undo almost anything you do while working in Excel, including any change you enter into a cell. To undo a change, click the Undo button on the Standard toolbar.

To undo an Undo (reinstate a change), click the Redo button in the Standard toolbar.

Undoing/Redoing More Than One Thing   Normally, when you click the Undo or Redo button, Excel undoes or repeats only the most recent action. To undo (or redo) an action prior to the most recent, click the drop-down arrow on the button and select the action you want from the list. In Excel 97, you can click the Undo button multiple times to undo a series of previous actions.

SELECTING CELLS

In order to copy, move, or delete the data in several cells at one time, you must select those cells first. Then you can perform the appropriate action.

- To select a single cell, click it.

- To select adjacent cells (a *range*), click the upper-left cell in the group and drag down to the lower-right cell to select additional cells. (If you want more help in selecting ranges of various sizes, see Lesson 10.)

- To select nonadjacent cells, press and hold the Ctrl key as you click individual cells.

- To select an entire row or column of cells, click the row or column header.

- To select adjacent rows or columns, drag over their headers.

- To select nonadjacent rows or columns, press Ctrl and click the headers for those you want to select.

Range   A selection of adjacent cells.

COPYING DATA

When you copy or move data, a copy of that data is placed in a temporary storage area called the *Clipboard*. You can copy data to other sections of your worksheet or to other worksheets or workbooks. When you copy, the original data remains in its place and a copy of it is placed where you indicate.

What Is the Clipboard?   The Clipboard is an area of memory that is accessible to all Windows programs. The Clipboard is used to copy or move data from place to place within a program or between programs. The techniques that you learn here are the same ones used in all Windows programs.

Follow these steps to copy data:

1. Select the cell(s) that you want to copy.

2. Click the Copy button on the Standard toolbar. The contents of the selected cell(s) are copied to the Clipboard.

3. Select the first cell in the area where you would like to place the copy. (To copy the data to another worksheet or workbook, change to that worksheet or workbook first.)

4. Click the Paste button. Excel inserts the contents of the Clipboard in the location of the insertion point.

Watch Out!   When copying or moving data, be careful not to paste the data over existing data (unless, of course, you intend to).

You can copy the same data to several places by repeating the Paste command. Data copied to the Clipboard remains there until you copy or cut (move) something else.

USING DRAG AND DROP

The fastest way to copy something is to drag and drop it. Select the cells you want to copy, hold down the Ctrl key, and drag the border of the range you selected (see Figure 6.2). When you release the mouse button, the contents are copied to the new location. (If you forget to hold down the Ctrl key, Excel moves the data instead of copying it.) To insert the data *between* existing cells, press Ctrl+Shift as you drag.

To drag a copy to a different sheet, press Ctrl+Alt as you drag the selection to the sheet's tab. Excel switches you to that sheet, where you can drop your selection in the appropriate location.

MOVING DATA

Moving data is similar to copying except that the data is removed from its original place and placed in the new location.

To move data, follow these steps:

1. Select the cells you want to move.

2. Click the Cut button.

3. Select the first cell in the area where you would like to place the data. To move the data to another worksheet, change to that worksheet.

4. Click Paste.

Drag the range by its border.   Outline shows where data will be copied.

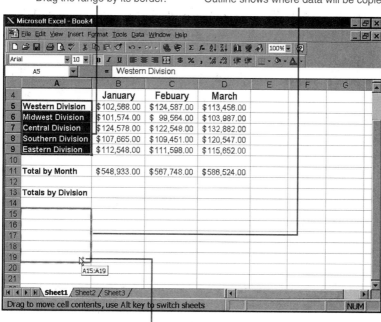

The plus sign shows that data will be copied, not moved.

FIGURE 6.2   To copy data, hold down the Ctrl key while dragging the cell selector border.

To move data quickly, use the drag and drop feature. Select the data to be moved, and then drag the border of the selected cells to its new location. To insert the data between existing cells, press Shift while you drag. To move the data to a different worksheet, press the Alt key and drag the selection to the worksheet's tab. You're switched to that sheet, where you can drop your selection at the appropriate point.

Shortcut Menu   When cutting, copying, and pasting data, don't forget the shortcut menu. Simply select the cells you want to cut or copy, *right-click*, and choose the appropriate command from the shortcut menu that appears.

DELETING DATA

To delete the data in a cell or cells, you can just select them and press Delete. However, Excel offers additional options for deleting cells:

- With the Edit, Clear command, you can delete just the formatting of a cell (or an attached comment), instead of deleting its contents. The formatting of a cell includes the cell's color, border style, numeric format, font size, and so on. You'll learn more about this option in a moment.

- With the Edit, Delete command, you can remove cells and everything in them. This option is covered in Lesson 13.

To use the Clear command to remove the formatting of a cell or a note, follow these steps:

1. Select the cells you want to clear.

2. Open the Edit menu and select Clear. The Clear submenu appears.

3. Select the desired clear option: All (which clears the cells of all contents, formatting, and notes), Formats, Contents, or Comments.

FINDING AND REPLACING DATA

With Excel's Find and Replace features, you can locate certain data and replace it with new data. When you have a label, a value, or formula that is entered incorrectly throughout the worksheet, you can use the Edit, Replace command to search and replace all occurrences of the incorrect information with the correct data.

To find and replace data, follow these steps:

1. Open the Edit menu and select Replace. The Replace dialog box appears, as shown in Figure 6.3.

Type the data you want to find.   Click here to find the next occurrence.

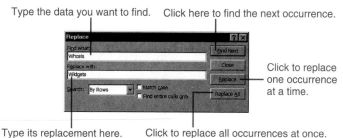

Type its replacement here.   Click to replace all occurrences at once.

Click to replace
one occurrence
at a time.

FIGURE 6.3   Find and replace data with the Replace dialog box.

2. Type the text you want to find in the Find What text box.

3. Click in the Replace With text box and type the text you want to use as replacement text.

4. In the Search box, indicate whether you want to search for your entry by rows or by columns.

5. If you want to match the exact case of your entry, click Match Case. If you want to locate cells that contain exactly what you entered (and no additional data), click Find Entire Cells Only.

6. Click Find Next to find the first occurrence of your specified text. Then click Replace to replace only this occurrence or Replace All to replace all occurrences of the data you specified.

In this lesson, you learned how to edit cell data and undo changes. In addition, you learned how to copy, move, and delete data. In the next lesson, you will learn how to work with workbook files.

CREATING AND SAVING WORKBOOK FILES

In this lesson you will learn how to create new workbooks and save workbook files.

CREATING A NEW WORKBOOK

You can create a new *blank* workbook, or you can use a template to create a more complete workbook. A *template* is a predesigned workbook that you can modify to suit your needs. Excel contains templates for creating invoices, expense reports, and other common worksheets.

Here's how you create a new workbook:

1. Pull down the File menu and select New. The New dialog box appears. As you can see in Figure 7.1, this dialog box contains two tabs: General and Spreadsheet Solutions.

2. To create a blank workbook, click the General tab and click the Workbook icon.

   To create a workbook from a template, click the Spreadsheet Solutions tab. You'll see icons for several common worksheet types. Click the icon for the type of workbook you want to create.

3. Once you've made your selection, click OK or press Enter. A new workbook opens on-screen with a default name in the title bar. Excel numbers its files sequentially. For example, if you already have Book1 open, the Workbook title bar will read **Book2**.

General tab   Spreadsheet Solutions tab

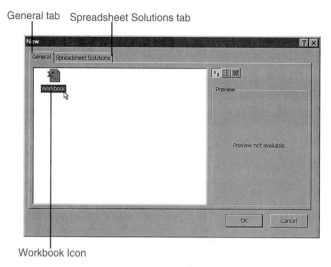

Workbook Icon

FIGURE 7.1   Click the icon for the type of worksheet you want to create.

 Instant Workbook   If you want to create a blank workbook (instead of creating one from a template), you can bypass the New dialog box by simply clicking the New button on the Standard toolbar. Excel opens a new workbook window without displaying the New dialog box.

 Fast Start   When you start Excel, you're normally given a blank worksheet to begin with. However, you can select a template instead. Just click the Start button on the Windows taskbar and select New Office Document. Excel displays the New Office Document dialog box. Click the Spreadsheet Solutions tab, select the type of workbook you want to create, and then click OK.

SAVING AND NAMING A WORKBOOK

Whatever you type into a workbook is stored only in your computer's temporary memory. If you exit Excel, that data will be lost. Therefore, it is important to save your workbook files to a disk regularly.

The first time you save a workbook to a disk, you have to name it. Follow these steps to name your workbook:

1. Open the File menu and select Save, or click the Save button on the Standard toolbar. The Save As dialog box appears (see Figure 7.2).

Select a drive and folder.   Click the Up One Level button to move up a folder level.

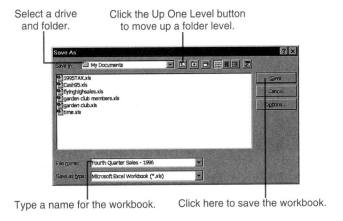

Type a name for the workbook.   Click here to save the workbook.

FIGURE 7.2   The Save As dialog box.

2. Type the name you want to give the workbook in the File Name text box. You can use up to 218 characters, including any combination of letters, numbers, and spaces (as in **Fourth Quarter Sales - 1996**).

3. Normally, Excel saves your workbooks in the My Documents folder. To save the file to a different folder, select it from the Save In list. You can move up a folder level by clicking the Up One Level button on the Save toolbar at

the top of the dialog box. You can change to a different drive by selecting a drive in the Save In box. When you save a file to any of the places listed in the Save In box, here's what happens:

- **Desktop**   Saves the file as an icon on the Windows desktop. Double-click the icon on your desktop to quickly start Excel and open the workbook file at the same time. If you're working on a project in Excel on a daily basis, you might want to have the file icon on the desktop for your convenience.

- **My Computer**   Saves the file to Windows' My Computer folder. Open the My Computer window and double-click the file icon to start Excel and open the workbook file. If you are working in My Computer regularly, it might be convenient to save the file to My Computer. You can also save your file to your hard drive or floppy drive in My Computer.

- **Network Neighborhood**   Saves the file to Windows' Network Neighborhood. Open Network Neighborhood and double-click the file icon to start Excel and open the workbook file. If you work in Network Neighborhood regularly, it might be convenient to save the file to Network Neighborhood.

4. Click the Save button or press Enter.

Excel on the Web   You can save your worksheet in HTML format and add it to your company's intranet (or Internet) Web site. See Lesson 21 for details.

Default Directory   Normally, files are saved to the My Documents directory. You can change the default to your own private directory if you want. Open the Tools menu, select Options, and click the General tab. Click in the Default File Location text box and type a complete path for the drive and directory you want to use (the directory must be an existing one). Click OK.

 To save a file you have saved previously (and named), all you do is click the Save button. (Or you can press Ctrl+S or use the File, Save command.) Excel automatically saves the workbook and any changes you entered without displaying the Save As dialog box.

-97. **Excel on the Web**   You can save your workbook to an FTP site on the Internet (or a local intranet), provided you have the permission to do so. First, to add the FTP site to the Save As dialog, open the Save In list and select Add/ Modify FTP Locations. In the Name of FTP Site text box, enter the site's address, such as **ftp://ftp.microsoft.com**. Select either Anonymous or User Login and enter a password if necessary. Click Add. Once the site has been added to the Save As dialog box, you can select it from the Internet Locations (FTP) folder in the Save In list.

SAVING A WORKBOOK UNDER A NEW NAME

Sometimes you might want to change a workbook but keep a copy of the original workbook, or you may want to create a new workbook by modifying an existing one. You can do this by saving the workbook under another name or in another folder. The following steps show how you do that:

1. Open the File menu and select Save As. You'll see the Save As dialog box, just as if you were saving the workbook for the first time.

2. To save the workbook under a new name, type the new file name over the existing name in the File Name text box.

3. To save the file on a different drive or in a different folder, select the drive letter or the folder from the Save In list.

4. To save the file in a different format (such as Lotus 1-2-3 or Quattro Pro), click the Save As Type drop-down arrow and select the desired format.

5. Click the Save button or press Enter.

 Backup Files   You can have Excel create a backup copy of each workbook file you save. That way, if anything happens to the original file, you can use the backup copy. To turn the backup feature on, click the Options button in the Save As dialog box, select Always Create Backup, and click OK. To use the backup file, choose File, Open to display the Open dialog box, and then select Backup Files from the Files of Type list. Double-click the backup file in the files and folders list to open the file.

In this lesson, you learned how to create new workbooks and save workbooks. In the next lesson, you'll learn how to open and close workbook files.

OPENING AND CLOSING WORKBOOK FILES

In this lesson you will learn how to open and close workbook files. You will also learn how to locate misplaced files.

OPENING AN EXISTING WORKBOOK

If you have closed a workbook and then later you want to use it again, you must reopen it. Follow these steps to open an existing workbook:

1. Open the File menu and select Open, or click the Open button on the Standard toolbar. The Open dialog box shown in Figure 8.1 appears.

Type the name of the file you want to open...

...or select the file from the list.

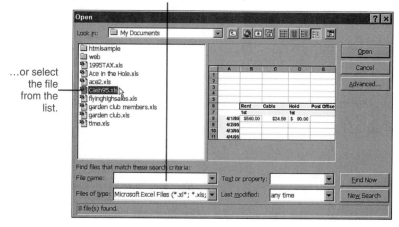

FIGURE 8.1   The Open dialog box.

2. If the file is not located in the current folder, open the
   Look In box and select the correct drive and folder.

Excel on the Web   To open a worksheet on an FTP site
to which you have access, select Internet Locations (FTP)
from the Look In box and double-click the FTP site you
want to search. Then click the workbook you want to open
and click Open. To search the Web for a worksheet
instead, click the Search the Web button at the top of
the Open dialog box.

3. Click the file you want to open in the files and folders
   list. Or, type the name of the file in the File Name box.
   (As you type, Excel highlights the first file name in the
   list that matches your entry; this is a quick way to move
   through the list.)

Save Your Favorites   You can save the worksheets you
use most often in the Favorites folder. Just select the
worksheet and click the Look in Favorites button. To open
one of those worksheets later, click the Look in Favorites
button at the top of the Open dialog box.

4. To see a preview of the workbook before you open it, click
   the Preview button at the top of the dialog box. Excel
   displays the contents of the workbook in a window to the
   right of the dialog box.

5. Click Open or press Enter.

Recently Used Workbooks   If you've recently used the
workbook you want to open, you'll find it listed at the bottom of the File menu. Just open the File menu and select
it from the list.

Excel on the Web   You can browse the Web for a worksheet with the Search the Web button. But if you know the exact address of the worksheet you want to open (whether it's on the Web or on a local intranet), you can just type its address (such as **http:// www.worldnews.com/facts.xls**) in the File Name text box. (You must connect to the Internet before you click Open.)

You can also open a specific workbook when you first start Excel. Just click the Start button on the Windows taskbar and select Open Office Document. Select the workbook you want to open and click Open. Excel starts, with the workbook you selected open and ready to edit.

FINDING A WORKBOOK FILE

If you forget where you saved a file, Excel can help you. You can use its Find Now option in the Open dialog box. Follow these steps to have Excel hunt for a file for you:

1. Open the File menu and select Open, or click the Open button in the Standard toolbar. The Open dialog box appears (see Figure 8.2).

2. Open the Look In box and select the drive and/or folder you want to search. For example, if you select C:, Excel will search the entire C drive. If you select C: and then select the Excel folder, Excel searches only the EXCEL directory on drive C. You can select My Computer to search all the drives on your computer.

3. Narrow your search using any of the following methods:

    If you want to search for a particular file, type its name in the File Name text box. You can use wild-card characters in place of characters you can't remember. Use an asterisk (*) in place of a group of characters; use a question mark (?) in place of a single character. (For example, if you enter **sales??**, Excel finds all files whose file names begin with the word "sales" followed by two characters, such as SALES01, SALES02, and so on.)

Select the drive and/or folder to search.   Click here to search all subfolders.

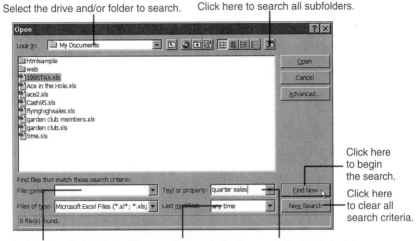

Click here
to begin
the search.

Click here
to clear all
search criteria.

Type the file name to look for.   Choose a time period.   Type specific text to look for.

FIGURE 8.2   The Search options in the Open dialog box enable you to specify what you want to search for.

You can search the contents of your workbooks for a particular phrase by typing it in the Text Or Property box. For example, type **"brook trout"** to find a workbook that contains the words "brook trout."

To specify a time period for the files you want to search, choose an option from the Last Modified box.

 To have Excel search all subfolders of the drive you specify, click the Commands and Settings button and choose Search Subfolders from the pop-up menu that appears.

 Do Over   You can clear your search selections by clicking the New Search button.

4. When you finish entering your search criteria, click the Find Now button. Excel finds the files that match the search instructions you entered and displays them in the files and folders list.

5. Look through the list, highlight the file you want, and click the Open button.

 File Not Found?   If the file you want is not listed in the files and folders list, you can specify more detailed search criteria by using the Advanced Find feature. Click the Advanced button in the Open dialog box. Enter search criteria such as property, condition, or value, and then click the Find Now button to search for the file using these additional criteria.

Moving Among Open Workbooks

Sometimes you may have more than one workbook open at a time. If so, you can switch back and forth as necessary to view or edit their contents. There are several ways to move among open workbooks:

- If part of the desired workbook window is visible, click it.

- Open the Window menu and select the name of the workbook to which you want to switch.

- Press Ctrl+F6 to move from one workbook window to another.

 The Active Window   If you have more than one workbook open, only the one where the cell selector is located is considered active. The title bar of the active workbook will be darker than the title bars of other open workbooks.

CLOSING WORKBOOKS

When you close a workbook, Excel removes its workbook window from the screen. You should close workbooks when you finish working on them to free up your computer's resources so it can respond to your commands more quickly. To close a workbook, follow these steps:

1. If the window you want to close isn't currently active, make it active by selecting the workbook from the list of workbooks at the bottom of the Window menu.

2. Click the Close (X) button in the upper-right corner of the workbook.

 Close All In Excel 97, if you have more than one workbook open, you can close all of them at once by holding down the Shift key, opening the File menu, and selecting Close All.

In this lesson, you learned how to open and close workbooks, as well as how to find misplaced workbook files. The next lesson teaches you how to work with the worksheets in a workbook.

*In this lesson, you learn how to add
and delete worksheets with workbooks.
You also learn how to copy, move,
and rename worksheets.*

SELECTING WORKSHEETS

By default, each workbook consists of three worksheet pages
whose names appear on tabs near the bottom of the screen. You
can insert new worksheet pages or delete worksheet pages as desired. One advantage to having multiple worksheet pages is to
organize your data into logical chunks. Another advantage to
having separate worksheets for your data is that you can reorga-
nize the worksheets in a workbook easily.

Before we get into the details of inserting, deleting, and copying
worksheets, you should know how to select one or more
worksheets. Here's what you need to know:

- To select a single worksheet, click its tab. The tab becomes
  highlighted to show that the worksheet is selected.

- To select several neighboring worksheets, click the tab of
  the first worksheet in the group, and then hold down the
  Shift key and click the tab of the last worksheet in the
  group.

- To select several non-neighboring worksheets, hold down
  the Ctrl key and click each worksheet's tab.

If you select two or more worksheets, they remain selected until
you ungroup them. To ungroup worksheets, do one of the following:

- Right-click one of the selected worksheets and choose Ungroup Sheets.

- Hold down the Shift key and click the active tab.

- Click any tab outside the group.

INSERTING WORKSHEETS

When you create a new workbook, it contains three worksheets. You can easily add additional worksheets to a workbook.

Start with More   You can change the number of worksheets Excel places in a new workbook by opening the Tools menu, selecting Options, clicking the General tab, and then changing the number under the Sheets in New Workbook option. Click OK to save your changes.

Follow these steps to add a worksheet to a workbook:

1. Select the worksheet *before* which you want the new worksheet inserted. For example, if you select Sheet2, the new worksheet (which will be called Sheet4 because the workbook already contains 3 worksheets) will be inserted before Sheet2.

2. Open the Insert menu.

3. Select Worksheet. Excel inserts the new worksheet, as shown in Figure 9.1.

Shortcut Menu   A faster way to work with worksheets is to right-click the worksheet tab. This brings up a shortcut menu that lets you insert, delete, rename, move, copy, or select all worksheets. When you choose Insert from the shortcut menu, Excel displays the Insert dialog box. Click the Worksheet icon on the General tab and click OK to insert a new worksheet.

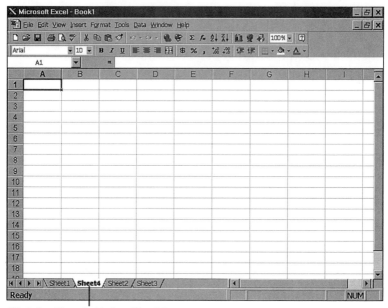

Worksheet inserted before Sheet 2

FIGURE 9.1 Excel inserts the new worksheet before the worksheet you selected.

DELETING WORKSHEETS

If you plan to use only one worksheet, you can remove the two other worksheets to free up memory. Here's how you remove a worksheet:

1. Select the worksheet(s) you want to delete.

2. Open the Edit menu.

3. Click Delete Sheet. A dialog box appears, asking you to confirm the deletion.

4. Click the OK button. The worksheets are deleted.

MOVING AND COPYING WORKSHEETS

You can move or copy worksheets within a workbook or from one workbook to another. Here's how:

1. Select the worksheet(s) you want to move or copy. If you want to move or copy worksheets from one workbook to another, be sure to open the target workbook.

2. Open the Edit menu and choose Move or Copy Sheet. The Move or Copy dialog box appears, as shown in Figure 9.2.

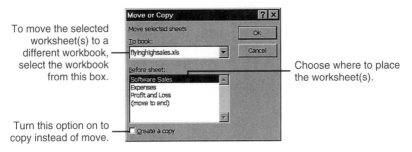

To move the selected worksheet(s) to a different workbook, select the workbook from this box.

Choose where to place the worksheet(s).

Turn this option on to copy instead of move.

FIGURE 9.2 The Move or Copy dialog box asks where you want to copy or move a worksheet.

3. To move the worksheet(s) to a different workbook, select that workbook's name from the To Book drop-down list. If you want to move or copy the worksheet(s) to a new workbook, select (new book) in the To Book drop-down list. Excel creates a new workbook and then copies or moves the worksheet(s) to it.

4. In the Before Sheet list box, choose the worksheet *before* which you want the selected worksheet(s) to be moved.

5. To copy the selected worksheet(s) instead of moving them, select Create a Copy to put a check mark in the check box.

6. Select OK. The selected worksheet(s) are copied or moved as specified.

MOVING A WORKSHEET WITHIN A WORKBOOK BY DRAGGING AND DROPPING

An easier way to copy or move worksheets within a workbook is to use the drag and drop feature. First, select the tab of the worksheet(s) you want to copy or move. Move the mouse pointer over one of the selected tabs, click and hold the mouse button, and drag the tab where you want it moved. To copy the worksheet, hold down the Ctrl key while dragging. When you release the mouse button, the worksheet is copied or moved.

MOVING A WORKSHEET BETWEEN WORKBOOKS BY DRAGGING AND DROPPING

You can also use the drag and drop feature to quickly copy or move worksheets between workbooks. First, open the workbooks you want to use for the copy or move. Choose Window, Arrange and select the Tiled option. Click OK to arrange the windows so that a small portion of each one appears on-screen. Select the tab of the worksheet(s) you want to copy or move. Move the mouse pointer over one of the selected tabs, click and hold the mouse button, and drag the tab where you want it moved. To copy the worksheet, hold down the Ctrl key while dragging. When you release the mouse button, the worksheet is copied or moved.

CHANGING WORKSHEET TAB NAMES

By default, all worksheets are named "Sheet$X$," where X is a number starting with the number 1. So that you'll have a better idea of the information each sheet contains, you can change the names that appear on the tabs. Here's how you do it:

1. Double-click the tab of the worksheet you want to rename. The current name is highlighted.

2. Type a new name for the worksheet and press Enter. Excel replaces the default name with the name you typed.

In this lesson, you learned how to insert, delete, move, copy, and rename worksheets. In the next lesson, you'll learn how to work with cell ranges.

LESSON 10

WORKING WITH RANGES

In this lesson, you will learn how to select and name cell ranges.

WHAT IS A RANGE?

A *range* is a rectangular group of connected cells. The cells in a range may all be in one column, or one row, or any combination of columns and rows, as long as the range forms a rectangle, as shown in Figure 10.1.

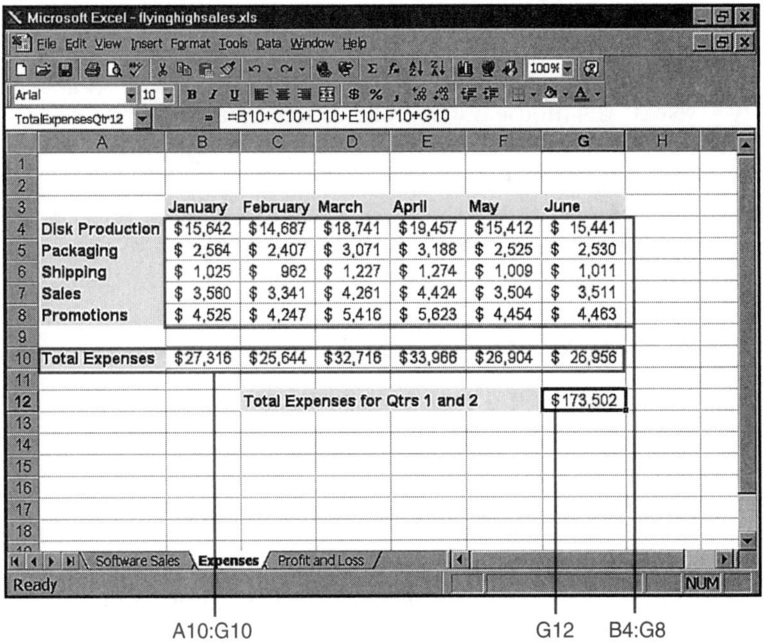
A10:G10
G12
B4:G8

FIGURE 10.1 A range is any combination of cells that forms a rectangle.

Learning how to use ranges can save you time. For example, you can select a range and use it to format a group of cells with one step. You can use a range to print only a selected group of cells. You can also use ranges in formulas.

Ranges are referred to by their anchor points (the upper-left corner and the lower-right corner). For example, the ranges shown in Figure 10.1 are B4:G8, A10:G10, and G12.

SELECTING A RANGE

To select a range using the mouse, follow these steps:

1. To select the same range of cells on more than one worksheet, select the worksheets (see Lesson 9).

2. Move the mouse pointer to the upper-left corner of a range.

3. Click and hold the left mouse button.

4. Drag the mouse to the lower-right corner of the range and release the mouse button. The selected range is high-lighted.

There are some techniques that you can use to quickly select a row, a column, an entire worksheet, or several ranges, as shown in Table 10.1.

TABLE 10.1   SELECTION TECHNIQUES

TO SELECT THIS	DO THIS
Several ranges	Select the first range, hold down the Ctrl key, and select the next range. Do this for each range you want to select.
Row	Click the row heading number at the left edge of the worksheet. You also can press Shift+Spacebar.

To Select This	Do This
Column	Click the column heading letter at the top edge of the worksheet. You also can press Ctrl+Spacebar.
Entire worksheet	Click the Select All button (the blank rectangle in the upper-left corner of the worksheet, above row 1 and left of column A). You also can press Ctrl+A.
Range that is out of view	Press Ctrl+G (Goto) or click in the Name box on the Formula bar, and type the address of the range you want to select. For example, to select the range R100 to T250, type **R100:T250** and press Enter.

Deselecting a Selection   To remove the range selection, click any cell in the worksheet.

Naming Cells and Cell Ranges

Up to this point, you have used cell addresses to refer to cells. Although that works, it is often more convenient to name cells with more recognizable names. For example, say you want to determine your net income by subtracting expenses from income (see Lesson 14). You can name the cell that contains your total income "INCOME,"and name the cell that contains your total expenses "EXPENSES." You can then determine your net income by using the formula:

= INCOME – EXPENSES

Giving the cells memorable names will make the formula more logical and easier to manage. Naming cells and ranges also makes it easier to cut, copy, and move blocks of cells, as explained in Lesson 6.

Follow these steps to name a cell range:

1. Select the range of cells you want to name. Make sure all the cells are on the same worksheet. (You cannot name cells and cell ranges that are located on more than one sheet.)

2. Click in the Name box on the left side of the Formula bar (see Figure 10.2).

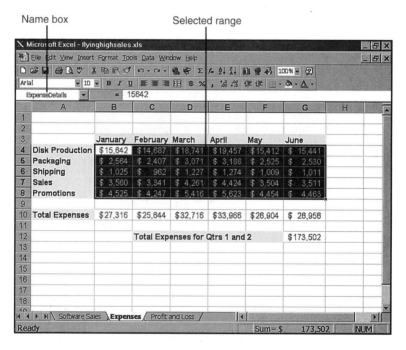

FIGURE 10.2 Type a name in the Name box.

3. Type a range name using up to 255 characters. Valid names can include letters, numbers, periods, and under-lines, but no spaces. In addition, a number cannot be used as the first character in the range name.

4. Press Enter.

5. To see the list of range names, click the Name box's drop-down arrow (on the Formula bar).

Another way to name a range is to select it, open the Insert menu, select Name, and choose Define. This displays the Define Name dialog box shown in Figure 10.3. Type a name in the Names in Workbook text box and click OK.

Type a name here.

Selected range appears here.

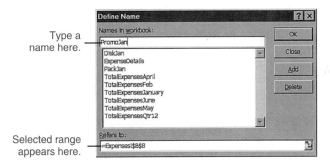

FIGURE 10.3 The Define Name dialog box.

The Define Name dialog box enables you to see what range a range name contains. Click a range name in the Names in Workbook list, and you'll see the cell address(es) assigned to the range name in the Refers To text box. You can edit the range or type a new one.

The dollar signs in the cell addresses indicate absolute cell references, which always refer to the same cell. An absolute cell reference will not be adjusted if changes are made to those cells in the worksheet (see Lesson 15). You don't have to type the dollar signs in the cell address. When you select cells with the mouse, Excel inserts the dollar signs automatically.

This dialog box also lets you delete names. To delete a range name, click a name in the Names in Workbook list and click the Delete button.

In this lesson, you learned how to select and name ranges. In the next lesson, you will learn how to print your workbook.

LESSON 11

PRINTING YOUR WORKBOOK

In this lesson, you will learn how to print an entire workbook or a portion of it.

CHANGING THE PAGE SETUP

A workbook is a collection of many worksheets, which are like pages in a notebook. You can print the whole notebook at once, or just one or more pages at a time.

Before you print a worksheet, you should make sure that the page is set up correctly for printing. To do this, open the File menu and choose Page Setup. You'll see the Page Setup dialog box shown in Figure 11.1.

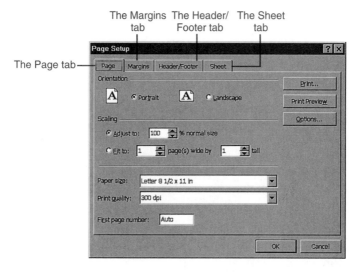

FIGURE 11.1 The Page Setup dialog box.

Right-Click the Workbook Title Bar For quick access to commands that affect a workbook, right-click on the workbook's title bar. If the workbook is maximized to a full screen (and the title bar is therefore not visible), right-click the Control-menu box to access the shortcut menu. For example, to check the page setup, right-click the title bar or the Control-menu box and choose Page Setup.

The following list outlines the page setup settings, grouped according to the tab on which they appear.

Page tab

> **Orientation** Select Portrait to print across the short edge of a page; select Landscape to print across the long edge of a page. (Landscape makes the page wider than it is tall.)
>
> **Scaling** You can reduce and enlarge your workbook or force it to fit within a specific page size (see Lesson 12).
>
> **Paper Size** This is 8 1/2 × 11 inches by default, but you can choose a different size from the list.
>
> **Print Quality** You can print your spreadsheet in draft quality to print quickly and save wear and tear on your printer, or you can print in high quality for a final copy. Print quality is measured in dpi (dots per inch); the higher the number, the better the print.
>
> **First Page Number** You can set the starting page number to something other than 1. The Auto option (default) tells Excel to set the starting page number to 1 if it is the first page in the print job, or to set the first page number at the next sequential number if it is not the first page in the print job.

Margins tab

> **Top, Bottom, Left, Right** You can adjust the size of the top, bottom, left, and right margins.

Header, Footer   You can specify how far you want a Header or Footer printed from the edge of the page. (You use the Header/Footer tab to add a header or footer to your workbook.)

Center on Page   You can center your workbook data between the left and right margins (Horizontally) and between the top and bottom margins (Vertically).

Header/Footer tab

Header, Footer   You can add a header (such as a title) that repeats at the top of each page, or a footer (such as page numbers) that repeats at the bottom of each page. See Lesson 12 for more information on headers and footers.

Custom Header, Custom Footer   You can use the Custom Header or Custom Footer button to create headers and footers that insert the time, date, worksheet tab name, and workbook file name.

Sheet tab

Print Area   You can print a portion of a workbook or worksheet by entering the range of cells you want to print. You can type the range, or click the Collapse Dialog Box icon at the right of the text box to move the Page Setup dialog box out of the way and drag the mouse pointer over the desired cells (see Lesson 12). If you do not select a print area, Excel will print either the sheet or the workbook, depending on the options set in the Page tab.

Don't Print That!   Ordinarily, if there's a portion of your worksheet that you don't want to print, you can avoid it by selecting the area you want to print and printing only that selection. However, if the data you want to hide is located *within* the area you want to print, what do you do? In that case, you can hide the columns, rows, or cells to prevent them from being printed. (See Lesson 2 for help.)

Print Titles   If you have a row or column of entries that you want repeated as titles on every page, type the range for this row or column, or drag over the cells with the mouse pointer (see Lesson 10).

Print   You can tell Excel exactly how to print some aspects of the workbook. For example, you can have the gridlines (the lines that define the cells) printed. You can also have a color spreadsheet printed in black-and-white.

Page Order   You can indicate how data in the worksheet should be read and printed: in sections from top to bottom or in sections from left to right. This is the way Excel handles printing the areas outside of the printable area. For example, if some columns to the right don't fit on the first page and some rows don't fit at the bottom of the first page, you can specify which area will print next.

When you finish entering your settings, click the OK button.

PREVIEWING A PRINT JOB

 After you've determined your page setup and print area, you should preview what the printed page will look like before you print. To preview a print job, open the File menu and select Print Preview or click the Print Preview button in the Standard toolbar. Your workbook appears as it will when printed, as shown in Figure 11.2.

> **Page Setup Print Preview**   You can also preview a print job when you are setting up a page or while you are in the Print dialog box. When the Page Setup dialog box is displayed, click the Print Preview button. In the Print dialog box, click the Preview button.

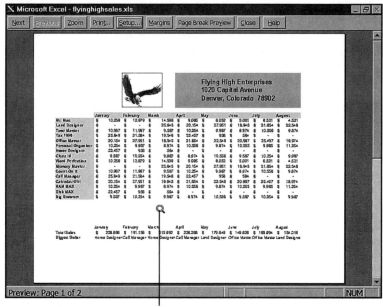

The mouse pointer allows you to zoom
in on a portion of the worksheet.

FIGURE 11.2   You can preview your workbook before printing it.

A Close-Up View   Zoom in on any area of the preview
by clicking on it with the mouse pointer (which looks like a
magnifying glass). You can also use the Zoom button at
the top of the Print Preview screen.

PRINTING YOUR WORKBOOK

After setting the page setup and previewing your data, it is time to
print. You can print selected data, selected sheets, or the entire
workbook.

To print your workbook, follow these steps:

1. If you want to print a portion of the worksheet, select the range you want to print (see Lesson 10 for help). If you want to print one or more sheets within the workbook, select the sheet tabs (see Lesson 9). To print the entire workbook, skip this step.

2. Open the File menu and select Print (or press Ctrl+P). The Print dialog box appears, as shown in Figure 11.3.

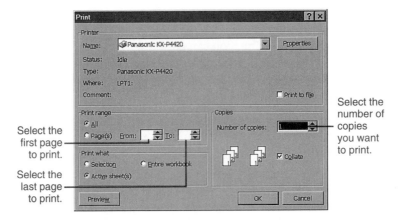

Select the first page to print.

Select the last page to print.

Select the number of copies you want to print.

FIGURE 11.3 The Print dialog box.

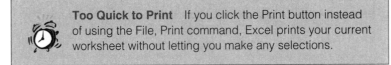

Too Quick to Print If you click the Print button instead of using the File, Print command, Excel prints your current worksheet without letting you make any selections.

3. Select the options you would like to use:

Page Range lets you print one or more pages. For example, if the selected print area will take up 15 pages and you want to print only pages 5–10, select Page(s), and then type the numbers of the first and last page you want to print in the From and To boxes.

Print What allows you to print the currently selected cells, the selected worksheets, or the entire workbook.

Copies allows you to print more than one copy of the selection, worksheet, or workbook.

Collate allows you to print a complete copy of the selection, worksheet, or workbook before the first page of the next copy is printed. This option is available when you print multiple copies.

4. Click OK or press Enter.

While your job is printing, you can continue working in Excel. If the printer is working on another job that you (or someone else, in the case of a network printer) sent, Windows holds the job until the printer is ready for it.

Sometimes you might want to delete a job while it is printing or before it prints. For example, suppose you think of other numbers to add to the worksheet or realize you forgot to format some text; you'll want to fix these things before you print the file. In such a case, deleting the print job is easy. To display the print queue and delete a print job, follow these steps:

1. Double-click the Printer icon on the Windows taskbar, and the print queue appears, as shown in Figure 11.4.

2. Click on the job you want to delete.

3. Open the Document menu and select Cancel Printing.

 Clear the Queue!   To delete all the files from the print queue, open the Printer menu and select Purge Print Jobs. This cancels the print jobs, but doesn't delete the files from your computer.

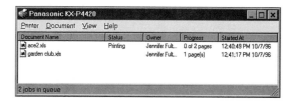

FIGURE 11.4   To stop a document from printing, use the print queue.

Upgrade Tip   With Excel 97, you get a newly expanded capability to send your worksheet directly to the people who need it, instead of printing it. Open the File menu, select Send To, and then select the appropriate option: Mail Recipient (to send a workbook via an e-mail message), Routing Recipient (route a workbook over a local network through Microsoft Mail or cc:Mail to several people), or Exchange Folder (to post—copy—your workbook to a Microsoft Exchange server).

In this lesson, you learned how to print all or part of your workbook. In the next lesson, you will learn how to print large worksheets.

12 LESSON

PRINTING LARGE WORKSHEETS

In this lesson, you will learn about the many aspects involved in printing a large worksheet.

SELECTING A PRINT AREA

You can tell Excel what part of the worksheet you want to print using the Print Area option. This option lets you single out an area as a separate page and then print that page. If the area is too large to fit on one page, Excel breaks it into multiple pages. If you do not select a print area, Excel prints either the entire worksheet or the entire workbook, depending on the options set in the Print dialog box.

To Include or Not to Include? When deciding which cells to select for your print area, make sure you do *not* include the title, the subtitle, and the column and row headings in the print area. If you do, Excel may print the labels twice. Instead, print your titles and headings on each page of your printout by following the steps in the upcoming section, "Printing Column and Row Headings."

To select a print area and print your worksheet at the same time, follow these steps:

1. Open the File menu and choose Page Setup. The Page Setup dialog box appears.

2. Click the Sheet tab to display the Sheet options.

3. Click the Collapse Dialog icon to the right of the Print Area text box. Excel reduces the Page Setup dialog box in size.

4. Drag over the cells you want to print (see Lesson 10). As you can see in Figure 12.1, a dashed line border surrounds the selected area, and the absolute cell references for those cells appear with dollar signs ($) in the Print Area text box. (If you want to type the range, you don't have to include the $ in the cell references. See Lesson 15 for more information about absolute cell references.)

5. Click the Collapse Dialog icon to return to the Page Setup dialog box.

6. Click Print in the Page Setup dialog box to display the Print dialog box. Then click OK to print your worksheet.

The addresses of the selected cells appear here.

Click the Collapse Dialog icon to return to the Page Setup dialog box.

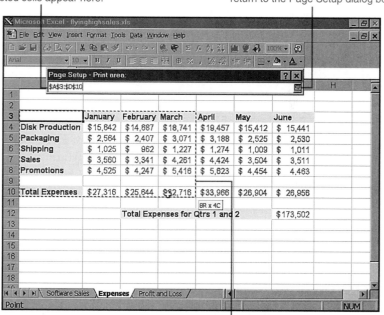

Drag over the desired cells.

FIGURE 12.1   Selecting a print area.

Set Your Area   To set the print area without printing, select the cells you want to print later, open the File menu, select Print Area, and select Set Print Area. To remove the print area, open the File menu, select Print Area, and select Clear Print Area.

ADJUSTING PAGE BREAKS

When you print a workbook, Excel determines the page breaks based on the paper size and margins and the selected print area. To make the pages look better and break information in logical places, you may want to override the automatic page breaks with your own breaks. However, before you add page breaks, try these options:

- Adjust the widths of individual columns to make the best use of space (see Lesson 20).

- Consider printing the workbook sideways (using Landscape orientation).

- Change the left, right, top, and bottom margins to smaller values.

If after trying these options you still want to insert page breaks, Excel 97 offers you an option of previewing exactly where the page breaks appear and then adjusting them. Follow these steps:

1. Open the View menu and select Page Break Preview.

2. If a message appears, click OK. Your worksheet is displayed with page breaks, as shown in Figure 12.2.

3. To move a page break, drag the dashed line to the desired location.

   To delete a page break, drag it off the screen.

   To insert a page break, move to the first cell in the column to the *right* of where you want the page break inserted, or move to the row *below* where you want the break inserted. For example, to insert a page break between columns G and H, move to cell H1. To insert a page break between rows 24 and 25, move to cell A25. Then open the Insert menu and select Page Break. A dashed line appears to the left of the selected column or above the selected row.

4. To exit Page Break Preview and return to your normal worksheet view, open the View menu and select Normal.

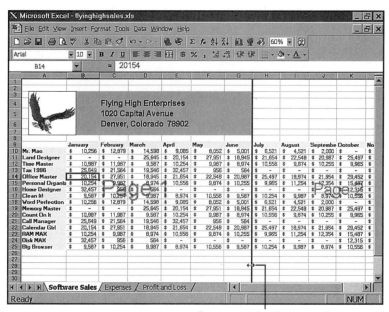

Drag a page break to move it.

FIGURE 12.2 Check your page breaks before printing.

PRINTING COLUMN AND ROW HEADINGS

Excel provides a way for you to select labels and titles that are located on the top edge and left side of a large worksheet, and print them on every page of the printout. This option is useful when a worksheet is too wide to print on a single page. If you don't use this option, the extra columns or rows will be printed on subsequent pages without any descriptive labels.

Follow these steps to print column or row headings on every page:

1. Open the File menu and choose Page Setup. The Page Setup dialog box appears.

2. Click the Sheet tab to display the Sheet options.

3. To repeat column labels and a worksheet title, click the Collapse Dialog icon to the right of the text box. Excel reduces the Page Setup dialog box in size.

4. Drag over the rows you want to print on every page, as shown in Figure 12.3. A dashed line border surrounds the selected area, and absolute cell references with dollar signs ($) appear in the Rows to Repeat at Top text box.

5. Click the Collapse Dialog icon to return to the Page Setup dialog box.

6. To repeat row labels that appear on the left of the worksheet, click the Collapse Dialog icon to the right of the text box. Again, Excel reduces the Page Setup dialog box.

7. Select the row labels you want to repeat.

8. Click the Collapse Dialog icon to return once again to the Page Setup dialog box.

9. To print your worksheet, click Print to display the Print dialog box. Then click OK.

 Select Your Print Area Carefully   If you select rows or columns to repeat, and those rows or columns are part of your print area, the selected rows or columns will print twice. To fix this, select your print area again, leaving out the rows or columns you're repeating. See "Selecting a Print Area" earlier in this lesson for help.

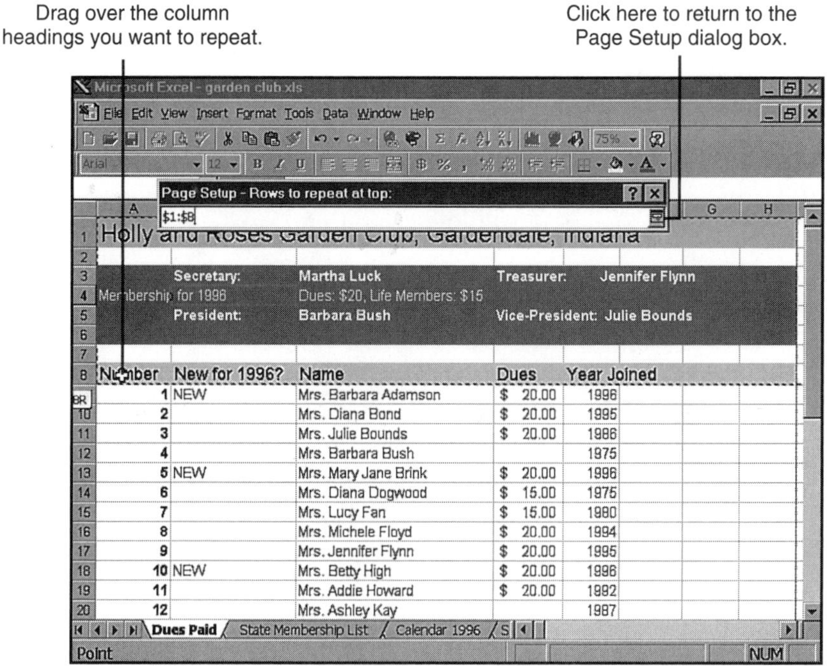

Drag over the column
headings you want to repeat.

Click here to return to the
Page Setup dialog box.

FIGURE 12.3   Specify the headings you want to print on every
page.

ADDING HEADERS AND FOOTERS

Excel lets you add headers and footers to print information at the
top and bottom of every page of the printout. The information
can include any text, as well as page numbers, the current date
and time, the workbook file name, and the worksheet tab name.

You can choose the headers and footers suggested by Excel, or
you can include any text plus special commands to control the
appearance of the header or footer. For example, you can apply
bold, italic, or underline to the header or footer text. You can also
left-align, center, or right-align your text in a header or footer (see
Lesson 18).

To add headers and footers, follow these steps:

1. Open the View menu and choose Header and Footer. The Page Setup dialog box appears (see Figure 12.4).

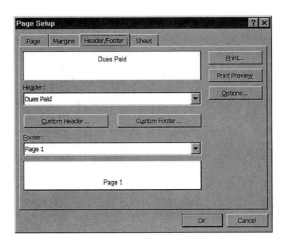

FIGURE 12.4 Adding headers and footers with Header/Footer options.

2. To select a header, click the Header drop-down arrow. Excel displays a list of suggested header information. Scroll through the list and click a header you want. The sample header appears at the top of the Header/Footer tab.

 Don't See One You Like? If none of the suggested headers or footers suit you, click the Custom Header or Custom Footer button and enter your own information.

3. To select a footer, click the Footer drop-down arrow. Excel displays a list of suggested footer information. Scroll through the list and click on a footer you want. The sample footer appears at the bottom of the Header/Footer tab.

4. Click OK to close the Page Setup dialog box and return to your worksheet. Or click the Print button to display the Print dialog box, and click OK to print your worksheet.

 Don't Want Any Headers or Footers? To remove the header and/or footer, choose (none) in the Header and/or Footer suggestions lists.

SCALING A WORKSHEET TO FIT ON A PAGE

If your worksheet is too large to print on one page even after you change the orientation and margins, you might consider using the Fit To option. This option shrinks the worksheet to make it fit on the specified number of pages. You can specify the document's width and height.

Follow these steps to scale a worksheet to fit on a page:

1. Open the File menu and choose Page Setup. The Page Setup dialog box appears.

2. Click the Page tab to display the Page options.

3. In the Fit to XX Page(s) Wide By and the XX Tall text boxes, enter the number of pages in which you want Excel to fit your data.

4. Click OK to close the Page Setup dialog box and return to your worksheet. Or click the Print button in the Page Setup dialog box to display the Print dialog box, and then click OK to print your worksheet.

In this lesson, you learned how to print a large worksheet. In the next lesson, you will learn how to add and remove cells, rows, and columns.

13 LESSON

INSERTING AND REMOVING CELLS, ROWS, AND COLUMNS

In this lesson, you will learn how to rearrange your worksheet by adding and removing cells, rows, and columns.

INSERTING CELLS

Sometimes you will need to insert information into a worksheet, right in the middle of existing data. With the Insert command, you can insert one or more cells or entire rows or columns.

 Shifting Cells Inserting cells in the middle of existing data will cause the data in existing cells to shift down a row or over a column. If your worksheet contains formulas that rely on the contents of the shifting cells, this could throw off the calculations (see Lessons 14 and 15). Double-check any formulas in your worksheet that might be affected.

To insert a single cell or a group of cells, follow these steps:

1. Select the cell(s) where you want the new cell(s) inserted. Excel will insert the same number of cells as you select.

2. Open the Insert menu and choose Cells. The Insert dialog box shown in Figure 13.1 appears.

3. Select Shift Cells Right or Shift Cells Down.

4. Click OK. Excel inserts the cell(s) and shifts the data in the other cells in the specified direction.

FIGURE 13.1   The Insert dialog box.

 Drag Insert   A quick way to insert cells is to hold down the Shift key and then drag the fill handle (the little box in the lower-right corner of the selected cell or cells—see Figure 13.2). Drag the fill handle up, down, left, or right to set the position of the new cells.

MERGING CELLS

In Excel 97, you can merge the data in one cell with other cells to form a big cell that is easier to work with. Merging cells is especially handy when creating a decorative title for the top of your worksheet (see Figure 13.2 for an example). Within a single merged cell, you can quickly change the font, point size, color and border style of your title. (See Lessons 17, 18, and 19 to learn more about formatting cells.)

To create a title with merged cells, follow these steps:

1. Type your title in the upper-left cell of the range you want to use for your heading. If you have a multi-line title, like the one in Figure 13.2, press Alt+Enter to insert each new line.

2. Select the range in which you want to place your title.

3. Open the Format menu and select Cells. The Format Cells dialog box appears.

4. Click the Alignment tab.

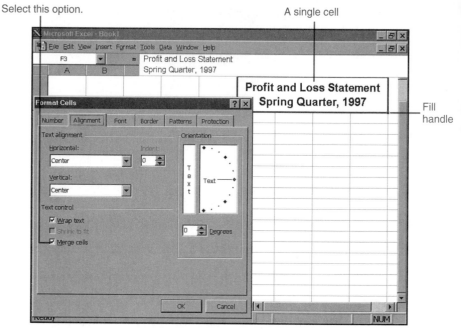

Select this option.

A single cell

Fill handle

FIGURE 13.2   Merge cells to form a single cell.

5. Click Merge Cells. You may also want to make adjustments to the text within the merged cells. For example, you may want to select Center in the Vertical drop-down list to center the text vertically within the cell.

6. Click OK when you're done. The selected cells are merged into a single cell, which you can format as needed.

You can merge selected cells and center the data in the leftmost cell by clicking the Merge and Center button on the Formatting toolbar.

REMOVING CELLS

In Lesson 6, you learned how to clear the contents and formatting of selected cells. That merely removed what was inside the cells. But sometimes you will want to eliminate the cells completely.

When you do, Excel removes the cells and adjusts the data in surrounding cells to fill the gap.

If you want to remove the cells completely, perform the following steps:

1. Select the range of cells you want to remove.

2. Open the Edit menu and choose Delete. The Delete dialog box appears.

3. Select the desired Delete option: Shift Cells Left or Shift Cells Up.

4. Click OK.

INSERTING ROWS AND COLUMNS

Inserting entire rows and columns in your worksheet is easy. Here's what you do:

1. *To insert a single row or column,* select the cell to the left of which you want to insert a column, or above which you want to insert a row.

   To insert multiple columns or rows, select the number of columns or rows you want to insert. To insert columns, drag over the column letters at the top of the worksheet. To insert rows, drag over the row numbers. For example, select three column letters or row numbers to insert three rows or columns.

2. Open the Insert menu.

3. Select Rows or Columns. Excel inserts the row(s) or column(s) and shifts the adjacent rows down or the adjacent columns right. The inserted rows or columns contain the same formatting as the cells you selected in step 1. Figure 13.3 simulates a worksheet before and after two rows were inserted.

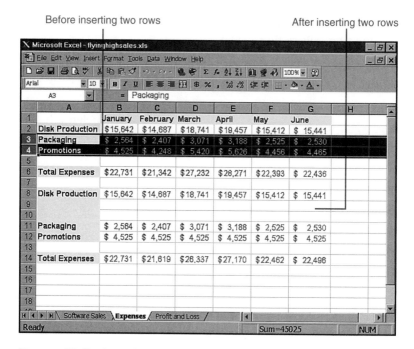

FIGURE 13.3   Inserting two rows in a worksheet.

Shortcut Insert   To quickly insert rows or columns, select one or more rows or columns. Then right-click one of them and choose Insert from the shortcut menu.

REMOVING ROWS AND COLUMNS

Deleting rows and columns is similar to deleting cells. When you delete a row, the rows below the deleted row move up to fill the space. When you delete a column, the columns to the right shift left.

Follow these steps to delete a row or column:

1. Click the row number or column letter of the row or column you want to delete. You can select more than one row or column by dragging over the row numbers or column letters.

2. Open the Edit menu and choose Delete. Excel deletes the row(s) or column(s) and renumbers the remaining rows and columns sequentially. All cell references in formulas and names in formulas are updated appropriately, unless they are absolute ($) values (see Lesson 15).

In this lesson, you learned how to insert and delete cells, rows, and columns. In the next lesson, you will learn how to use formulas.

PERFORMING CALCULATIONS WITH FORMULAS

In this lesson, you will learn how to use formulas to calculate results in your worksheets.

WHAT IS A FORMULA?

Worksheets use formulas to perform calculations on the data you enter. With formulas, you can perform addition, subtraction, multiplication, and division using the values contained in various cells.

Formulas typically consist of one or more cell addresses or values and a mathematical operator, such as + (addition), – (subtraction), * (multiplication), or / (division). For example, if you want to determine the average of the three values contained in cells A1, B1, and C1, you would type the following formula in the cell where you want the result to appear:

=(A1+B1+C1)/3

 Start Right Every formula must begin with an equal sign (=).

Figure 14.1 shows several formulas in action. Study the formulas and their results. Table 14.1 lists the mathematical operators you can use to create formulas.

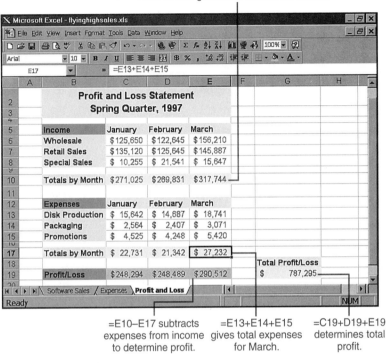

=E6+E7+E8 gives total income for March.

=E10–E17 subtracts expenses from income to determine profit.

=E13+E14+E15 gives total expenses for March.

=C19+D19+E19 determines total profit.

FIGURE 14.1   Type a formula in the cell where you want the resulting value to appear.

TABLE 14.1   EXCEL'S MATHEMATICAL OPERATORS

OPERATOR	PERFORMS	SAMPLE FORMULA	RESULT
^	Exponentiation	=A1^3	Enters the result of raising the value in cell A1 to the third power.
+	Addition	=A1+A2	Enters the total of the values in cells A1 and A2.

continues

TABLE 14.1   CONTINUED

OPERATOR	PERFORMS	SAMPLE FORMULA	RESULT
−	Subtraction	=A1−A2	Subtracts the value in cell A2 from the value in cell A1.
*	Multiplication	=A2*3	Multiplies the value in cell A2 by 3.
/	Division	=A1/50	Divides the value in cell A1 by 50.
	Combination	=(A1+A2+A3)/3	Determines the average of the values in cells A1 through A3.

ORDER OF OPERATIONS

Excel performs the operations within a formula in the following order:

1st	Exponential and equations within parentheses
2nd	Multiplication and division
3rd	Addition and subtraction

For example, given the formula =C2+B8*4+D10, Excel computes the value of B8*4, then adds that to C2, and then adds D10. Keep this order of operations in mind when you are creating equations because it determines the result.

If you don't take this order into consideration, you could run into problems when entering your formulas. For example, if you want to determine the average of the values in cells A1, B1, and C1, and you enter =A1+B1+C1/3, you'll get the wrong answer. The value in C1 will be divided by 3, and that result will be added to A1+B1.

To determine the total of A1 through C1 first, you must enclose that group of values in parentheses, as in =(A1+B1+C1)/3.

ENTERING FORMULAS

You can enter formulas in either of two ways: by typing the formula or by selecting cell references. To type a formula, perform the following steps:

1. Select the cell in which you want the formula's calculation to appear.

2. Type the equal sign (=).

3. Type the formula. The formula appears in the Formula bar.

4. Press Enter or click the Enter button (the check mark), and Excel calculates the result.

 Unwanted Formula If you start to enter a formula and then decide you don't want to use it, you can skip entering the formula by pressing Esc or clicking the Cancel button on the Formula bar (the one with the X).

Name That Cell If you plan to use a particular cell in several formulas, you can give it a name, such as "Income." Then you can use the name in the formula, as in =Income+$12.50. To name a cell, use the Insert, Name, Define command.

To enter a formula by selecting cell references, take the following steps:

1. Select the cell in which you want the formula's result to appear.

2. Type the equal sign (=).

3. Click the cell whose address you want to appear first in the formula. The cell address appears in the Formula bar.

 Upgrade Tip You can refer to a cell in a different worksheet by switching to that sheet and clicking the cell. To refer to a cell in a different workbook, open the workbook and click the cell. In Excel 97, the workbook to which you refer can even be located on the Internet or an intranet.

4. Type a mathematical operator after the value to indicate the next operation you want to perform. The operator appears in the Formula bar.

5. Continue clicking cells and typing operators until the formula is complete.

6. Press Enter to accept the formula or Esc to cancel the operation.

 Error! If **ERR** appears in a cell, make sure that you did not commit one of these common errors: try to divide by zero, use a blank cell as a divisor, refer to a blank cell, delete a cell used in a formula, or include a reference to the cell in which the answer appears.

 Natural Language Formulas Excel 97 now lets you refer to row and column headings (labels) when entering a formula. For example, if you had a worksheet with the row headings "Revenues," "Expenses," and "Profit," and you had column headings for each month, you could enter a formula such as =Jan Profit+Feb Profit or =Revenues–Expenses.

CALCULATING RESULTS WITHOUT ENTERING A FORMULA

You can view the sum of a range of cells simply by selecting the cells and looking at the status bar, as shown in Figure 14.2. You can also view the average, minimum, maximum, and the count of a range of cells. To do so, right-click the status bar and select the option you want from the shortcut menu that appears.

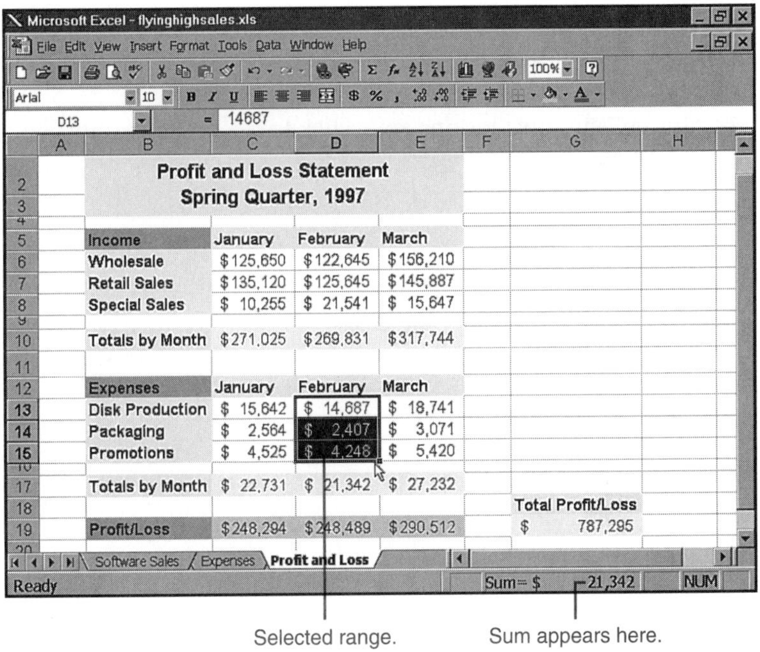

Selected range.   Sum appears here.

FIGURE 14.2   View a sum without entering a formula.

Where's the Status Bar?   If the status bar is not visible on your screen, you can display it by opening the View menu and clicking Status Bar.

DISPLAYING FORMULAS

Normally, Excel does not display the actual formula in a cell. Instead, it displays the result of the calculation. You can view the formula by selecting the cell and looking in the Formula bar. However, if you're trying to review the formulas in a large worksheet, it might be easier if you could see them all at once (or print them). If you want to view formulas in a worksheet, follow these steps:

1. Open the Tools menu and choose Options.
2. Click the View tab.
3. In the Window Options area, click to select the Formulas check box.
4. Click OK.

 Display Formulas Quickly   You can use a keyboard shortcut to toggle between viewing formulas and viewing values. To do so, hold down the Ctrl key and press ' (the accent key to the left of the 1 key; it has the tilde (~) on it). When you no longer need to view formulas, press Ctrl + ' again.

EDITING FORMULAS

Editing a formula is the same as editing any entry in Excel. Here's how you do it:

1. Select the cell that contains the formula you want to edit.
2. Click in the Formula bar or press F2 to enter Edit mode.

 Quick In-Cell Editing   To quickly edit the contents of a cell, double-click the cell. The insertion point appears inside the cell, and you can make any necessary changes.

3. Press the left arrow key (←) or right arrow key (→) to move the insertion point. Then use the Backspace key to delete characters to the left, or use the Delete key to delete characters to the right. Type any additional characters.

 4. When you finish editing the data, click the Enter button (the check mark) on the Formula bar or press Enter to accept your changes.

Another way to edit a formula is to click the Edit Formula button (the = sign) on the Formula bar. When you do, the Formula bar expands to provide you with help. Make your changes to the formula and then click OK.

In this lesson, you learned how to enter and edit formulas. In the next lesson, you will learn how to copy formulas, when to use relative and absolute cell addresses, and how to change Excel's settings for calculating formulas in the worksheet.

15

LESSON

COPYING FORMULAS AND RECALCULATING

In this lesson, you will learn how to copy formulas, use relative and absolute cell references, and change calculation settings.

COPYING FORMULAS

When you copy a formula, the formula is adjusted to fit the location of the cell to which it is copied. For example, if you copy the formula =C2+C3 from cell C4 to cell D4, the formula is adjusted for column D: it becomes =D2+D3. This allows you to copy similar formulas (such as the totals for a range of sales items) into a range of cells.

You can copy formulas using the Copy and Paste buttons (see Lesson 6), but there's a faster way.

1. Click the cell that contains the formula you want to copy.

2. Press Ctrl and drag the cell's border to the cell to which you want to copy your formula.

3. Release the mouse button, and Excel copies the formula to the new location.

If you want to copy a formula to a neighboring range of cells, follow these steps:

1. Click the cell that contains the formula you want to copy.

2. Move the mouse pointer over the fill handle.

3. Drag the fill handle across the cells into which you want to copy the formula.

Fast Copy   If you want to enter the same formula into a range of cells, select the range first. Then type the formula for the first cell in the range and press Ctrl+Enter.

Get an Error?   If you get an error after copying a formula, verify the cell references in the copied formula. See the next section, "Using Relative and Absolute Cell Addresses," for more details.

USING RELATIVE AND ABSOLUTE CELL ADDRESSES

When you copy a formula from one place in the worksheet to another, Excel adjusts the cell references in the formulas relative to their new positions in the worksheet. For example, in Figure 15.1, cell B8 contains the formula =B2+B3+B4+B5+B6, which computes the total expenses for January. If you copy that formula to cell C8 (to determine the total expenses for February), Excel automatically changes the formula to =C2+C3+C4+C5+C6. This is how relative cell addresses work.

Sometimes you may not want the cell references to be adjusted when you copy formulas. That's when absolute cell references become important.

Absolute versus Relative   An *absolute reference* is a cell reference in a formula that does not change when copied to a new location. A *relative reference* is a cell reference in a formula that is adjusted when the formula is copied.

Cell references are adjusted for column C.

	A	B	C	D	E	F	G
1		January	February	March	April	May	June
2	Disk Production	$ 15,642	$ 14,687	$18,741	$19,457	$15,412	$ 15,44
3	Shipping	$ 1,564	$ 1,469	$ 1,874	$ 1,946	$ 1,541	$ 1,54
4	Handling	$ 1,125	$ 1,056	$ 1,347	$ 1,398	$ 1,107	$ 1,10
5	Packaging	$ 2,564	$ 2,407	$ 3,071	$ 3,188	$ 2,525	$ 2,55
6	Promotions	$ 4,525	$ 4,248	$ 5,420	$ 5,626	$ 4,456	$ 4,46
7							
8	Total Expenses for the Month	$ 25,420	$ 23,867	$30,453	$31,615	$25,041	$ 25,08
9							
10	Total Expenses Qtrs 1 and 2	$161,485					
11							
12	Percentage of Total Expenses	16%	15%	19%	20%	16%	18
13							
14							
15							
16							
17							
18							

FIGURE 15.1 Excel adjusts cell references when you copy formulas to different cells.

In the example shown in Figure 15.1, the formulas in cells B12, C12, D12, E12, F12, and G12 contain an absolute reference to cell B10, which holds the total expenses for quarters 1 and 2. (The formulas in B12, C12, D12, E12, F12, and G12 divide the sums from row 8 of each column by the contents of cell B10.) If you didn't use an absolute reference, when you copied the formula from B10 to C10, the cell reference would be incorrect, and you would get an error message.

To make a cell reference in a formula absolute, you add a $ (dollar sign) before the letter and number that make up the cell address. For example, the formula in B12 would read as follows:

=B8/B10

You can type the dollar signs yourself, or you can press F4 after typing the cell address.

Some formulas use mixed references. For example, the column letter might be an absolute reference, and the row number might be a relative reference, as in the formula $A2/2. If you entered this formula in cell C2 and then copied it to cell D10, the result would be the formula $A10/2. The row reference (row number) would be adjusted, but the column reference (the letter A) would not be.

Mixed References   A reference that is only partially absolute, such as A$2 or $A2. When a formula that uses a mixed reference is copied to another cell, part of the cell reference (the relative part) is adjusted.

CHANGING THE CALCULATION SETTING

Excel recalculates the formulas in a worksheet every time you edit a value in a cell. However, on a large worksheet, you may not want Excel to recalculate until you have entered all of your changes. For example, if you are entering a lot of changes to a worksheet that contains many formulas, you can speed up the response time by changing from automatic to manual recalculation. To change the recalculation setting, take the following steps:

1. Open the Tools menu and choose Options.

2. Click the Calculation tab to see the options shown in Figure 15.2.

3. Select one of the following Calculation options:

   Automatic   This is the default setting. It recalculates the entire workbook each time you edit or enter a formula.

   Automatic Except Tables   This automatically recalculates everything except formulas in a data table. You'll learn about data tables (databases) in Lesson 25.

Manual   This option tells Excel to recalculate only when you say so. To recalculate, you press F9 or choose the Tools, Options, Calculation command and click the Calc Now button. When this option is selected, you can turn the Recalculate Before Save option off or on.

4. Click OK.

Calculation options —

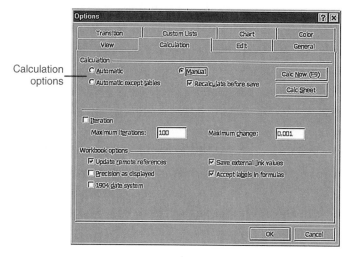

FIGURE 15.2   Change your calculation setting in the Options dialog box.

In this lesson, you learned how to copy formulas. You also learned when to use relative and absolute cell addresses and how to change calculation settings. In the next lesson, you will learn how to use Excel's Function Wizard to insert another type of formula, called a *function*.

PERFORMING CALCULATIONS WITH FUNCTIONS

In this lesson, you will learn how to perform calculations with functions and how to use Excel's Function Wizard to quickly insert functions in cells.

WHAT ARE FUNCTIONS?

Functions are complex ready-made formulas that perform a series of operations on a specified range of values. For example, to determine the sum of a series of numbers in cells A1 through H1, you can enter the function =SUM(A1:H1) instead of entering =A1+B1+C1 and so on. Functions can use range references (such as B1:B3), range names (such as SALES), or numerical values (such as 585.86).

Every function consists of the following three elements:

- The = sign indicates that what follows is a function (formula).

- The function name, such as SUM, indicates which operation will be performed.

- The argument, such as (A1:H1), indicates the cell addresses of the values that the function will act on. The argument is often a range of cells, but it can be much more complex.

You can enter functions either by typing them in cells or by using the Function Wizard, as you'll see later in this lesson. Table 16.1 shows Excel's most common functions that you'll use most in your worksheets.

Table 16.1   Excel's Most Common Functions

Function	Example	Description
AVERAGE	=AVERAGE(B4:B9)	Calculates the mean or average of a group of numbers.
COUNT	=COUNT(A3:A7)	Counts the numeric values in a range. For example, if a range contains some cells with text and other cells with numbers, you can count how many numbers are in that range.
COUNTA	=COUNTA(B4:B10)	Counts all cells in a range that are not blank. For example, if a range contains some cells with text and other cells with numbers, you can count how many cells in that range contain text.
IF	=IF(A3>=100, A3*2, A2*2)	Allows you to place a condition on a formula. In this example, if A3 is greater than or equal to 100, the formula A3*2 is used. If A3 is less than 100, the formula A2*2 is used instead.
MAX	=MAX(B4:B10)	Returns the maximum value in a range of cells.
MIN	=MIN(B4:B10)	Returns the minimum value in a range of cells.
PMT	=PMT(rate,nper,pv)	Calculates the periodic payment on a loan when you enter the interest rate, number of periods, and principal as arguments. Example: =PMT(.0825/12,360,180000) for 30 year loan at 8.25% for $180,000.

FUNCTION	EXAMPLE	DESCRIPTION
PMT	=PMT(rate, nper,, fv)	Calculates the deposit needed each period to reach some future value. Example: =PMT(.07/12,60,,10000) calculates the deposit needed to accumulate $10,000 at an annual rate of 7 percent, making monthly payments for five years (60 months).
SUM	=SUM(A1:A10)	Calculates the total in a range of cells.
SUMIF	=SUMIF(rg,criteria, sumrg)	Calculates the total of the range *rg* for each corresponding cell in *sumrg* that matches specified criteria. For example, =SUMIF (A2:A4,>100,B2:B4) adds the cells in the range A2:A4 whose corresponding cell in column B is greater than 100.

Excel on the Web   A new function, =HYPERLINK(), is used to create links to Web sites right in your worksheet. For example, =HYPERLINK(http://www.microsoft.com,"Visit Microsoft") will display the words "Visit Microsoft" in a cell. When the user clicks the cell, he or she is connected to the Microsoft home page. You can also use this feature to link to worksheets on your company's intranet.

Enter Text Right   When entering text into a formula, be sure to surround it with quotation marks, as in "Seattle."

Using AutoSum

Because SUM is one of the most commonly used functions, Excel provides a fast way to enter it—you simply click the AutoSum button in the Standard toolbar. Based on the currently selected cell, AutoSum guesses which cells you want summed. If AutoSum selects an incorrect range of cells, you can edit the selection.

To use AutoSum, follow these steps:

1. Select the cell in which you want the sum inserted. Try to choose a cell at the end of a row or column of data; doing so will help AutoSum guess which cells you want added together.

2. Click the AutoSum button in the Standard toolbar. AutoSum inserts =SUM and the range address of the cells to the left of or above the selected cell (see Figure 16.1).

3. If the range Excel selected is incorrect, drag over the range you want to use, or click in the Formula bar and edit the formula.

4. Click the Enter button in the Formula bar or press Enter. Excel calculates the total for the selected range.

>
> **Quickie AutoSum**   To quickly insert the SUM function, select the cell in which you want the sum inserted and double-click the AutoSum tool on the Standard toolbar. When you double-click the AutoSum button instead of single-clicking, you bypass the step where Excel displays the SUM formula and its arguments in the cell. Instead, you see the total in the cell and the SUM formula in the Formula bar. Of course, the problem with using this method is that you're not given a chance to "second-guess" the range of cells AutoSum decides to add.

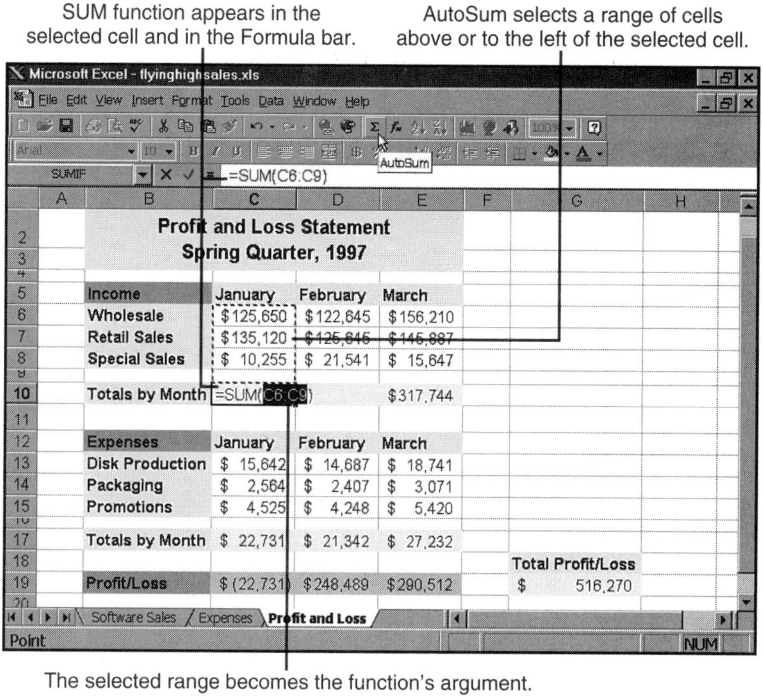

SUM function appears in the
selected cell and in the Formula bar.

AutoSum selects a range of cells
above or to the left of the selected cell.

The selected range becomes the function's argument.

FIGURE 16.1   AutoSum inserts the SUM function and selects the cells it plans to total.

USING AUTOCALCULATE

When you wanted to quickly check a total in earlier versions of Excel, did you ever use a calculator or enter temporary formulas on a worksheet? If you did, you might find Excel's AutoCalculate feature very handy. AutoCalculate lets you quickly check a total or an average, count entries or numbers, and find the maximum or minimum number in a range.

Here's how AutoCalculate works. To check a total, select the range you want to sum. Excel automatically displays the answer in the AutoCalculate area (as shown in Figure 16.2). If you want to perform a different function on a range of numbers, select the range and right-click in the AutoCalculate area to display the shortcut menu. Then choose a function from the menu. For example, choose Count to count the numeric values in the range. The answer appears in the AutoCalculate area.

AutoCalculate area

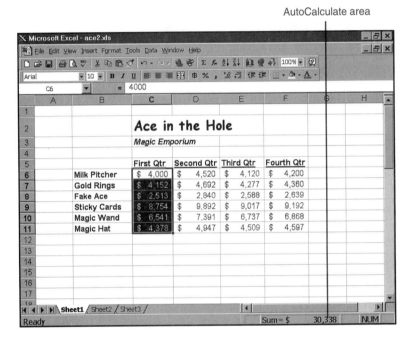

FIGURE 16.2   AutoCalculate lets you quickly view a sum.

> **Where's My Status Bar?**   If the status bar is not displayed, open the View menu and click the Status Bar.

USING THE FUNCTION WIZARD

Although you can type a function directly into a cell just as you can type formulas, you may find it easier to use the Function

Wizard. The Function Wizard leads you through the process of inserting a function. The following steps walk you through using the Function Wizard:

1. Select the cell in which you want to insert the function. (You can insert a function by itself or as part of a formula.)

2. Type = or click the Edit Formula button on the Formula bar. The Formula Palette appears, as shown in Figure 16.3.

Formula   Functions   Collapse Dialog
Palette   list   button

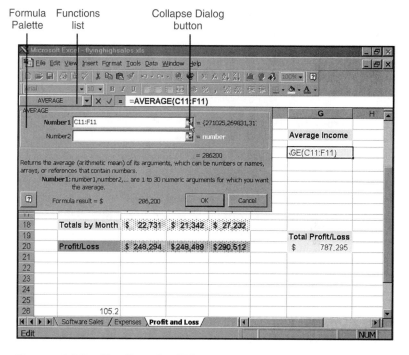

FIGURE 16.3   The Function Wizard helps you enter functions.

3. Select the function you want to insert from the Functions list by clicking the Functions button (see Figure 16.3). If you don't see your function listed, select More Functions at the bottom of the list.

What's This Function? If you don't know a lot about a particular function and you'd like to know more, click the Help button in the Formula Palette. When the Office Assistant appears, click Help with the Feature. Then click Help on Selected Function.

4. Enter the arguments for the formula. If you want to select a range of cells as an argument, click the Collapse Dialog button shown in Figure 16.3.

5. After selecting a range, click the Collapse Dialog button again to return to the Formula Palette.

6. Click OK. Excel inserts the function and argument in the selected cell and displays the result.

To edit a function, click the Edit Formula button. The Formula Palette appears. Change the arguments as needed and click OK.

In this lesson, you learned the basics of dealing with functions, and you learned how to use Excel's Function Wizard to quickly enter functions. You also learned how to quickly total a series of numbers with the AutoSum tool and how to check the sum of numbers with AutoCalculate. In the next lesson, you will learn how to format values in your worksheet.

Changing How Numbers Look

In this lesson, you will learn how to customize the appearance of numbers in your worksheet.

Formatting Values

Numeric values are usually more than just numbers. They represent a dollar value, a date, a percent, or some other value. Excel offers a wide range of number formats, which are listed in Table 17.1.

TABLE 17.1 EXCEL'S NUMBER FORMATS

NUMBER FORMAT	EXAMPLES	DESCRIPTION
General	10.6 $456,908.00	Excel displays your value as you enter it. In other words, this format displays currency or percent signs only if you enter them yourself.
Number	3400.50 (–120.39)	The default Number format has two decimal places. Negative numbers appear in red and in parentheses, pre ceded by a minus sign.

continues

TABLE 17.1   CONTINUED

NUMBER FORMAT	EXAMPLES	DESCRIPTION
Currency	$3,400.50 ($3,400.50)	The default Currency format has two decimal places and a dollar sign. Negative numbers appear in red and in parentheses.
Accounting	$ 3,400.00 $ 978.21	Use this format to align dollar signs and decimal points in a column. The default Accounting format has two decimal places and a dollar sign.
Date	11/7	The default Date format is the month and day separated by a slash; however, you can select from numerous other formats.
Time	10:00	The default Time format is the hour and minutes separated by a colon; however, you can opt to display seconds, AM, or PM.
Percentage	99.50%	The default Percentage format has two decimal places. Excel multiplies the value in a cell by 100 and displays the result with a percent sign.
Fraction	1/2	The default Fraction format is up to one digit on either side of the slash. Use this format to display the number of

NUMBER FORMAT	EXAMPLES	DESCRIPTION
		digits you want on either side of the slash and the fraction type (such as halves, quarters, eighths, and so on).
Scientific	3.40E+03	The default Scientific format has two decimal places. Use this format to display numbers in scientific notation.
Text	135RV90	Use Text format to display both text and numbers in a cell as text. Excel displays the entry exactly as you type it.
Special	02110	This format is specifically designed to display ZIP codes, phone numbers, and Social Security numbers correctly, so that you don't have to enter any special characters, such as hyphens.
Custom	00.0%	Use Custom format to create your own number format. You can use any of the format codes in the Type list and then make changes to those codes. The # symbol represents a number placeholder, and 0 represents a zero placeholder.

After deciding on a suitable numeric format, follow these steps:

1. Select the cell or range that contains the values you want to format.

2. Open the Format menu and select Cells. The Format Cells dialog box appears, as shown in Figure 17.1.

3. Click the Number tab.

4. In the Category list, select the numeric format category you want to use. The sample box displays the default format for that category.

5. Make changes to the format as needed.

6. Click OK or press Enter. Excel reformats the selected cells based on your selections.

Select a category.

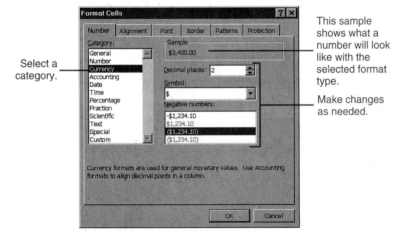

This sample shows what a number will look like with the selected format type.

Make changes as needed.

Figure 17.1   The Format Cells dialog box with the Number tab displayed.

 Removing Formatting   If you want to remove a number format from a cell (and return it to General format), select the cell whose formatting you want to remove, open the Edit menu, select Clear, and select Formats.

USING THE STYLE BUTTONS TO FORMAT NUMBERS

The Formatting toolbar (just below the Standard toolbar) contains several buttons for selecting a number format, including the following:

BUTTON	NAME	EXAMPLE/DESCRIPTION
$	Currency Style	$1200.90
%	Percent Style	20.90%
,	Comma Style	1,200.90
+.0 .00	Increase Decimal	Adds one decimal place
.00 +.0	Decrease Decimal	Deletes one decimal place

To use one of these buttons, select the cell you want to format and then click the desired button. You can also change the Number format of a cell by using the shortcut menu. Select the cell, right-click to display the shortcut menu, and choose Format Cells.

That's Not the Date I Entered!   If you enter a date in a cell that is formatted with the Number format, the date will appear as a number. With the Number format, Excel converts the date to a value that represents the number of days between January 1, 1900 and that date. For example, 01/01/1900 equals 1, and 12/31/1900 equals 366 (1900 was a leap year). To fix your problem, change the cell's formatting from Number format to Date format and select a date type.

Upgrade Tip   If you want to highlight cells that meet certain conditions, such as all values that are larger than 1,000, use conditional formatting. See Lesson 19 for more information.

CREATING YOUR OWN CUSTOM FORMAT

If you need to enter special numbers, such as account numbers, you might want to create your own number format and use it to format your account numbers. For example, suppose your account numbers look like this:

   10-20190-109

You could create a format like this:

   ##-#####-###

Then when you enter the number, 9089212098, for example, Excel formats it for you, adding the hyphens where needed:

   90-89212-098

Mixed Metaphors   Unfortunately, you can't create a format for a value that includes both text and numbers combined.

To create your own format, follow these steps:

1. Open the Format menu and select Cells.

2. Click the Number tab.

3. In the Category list, select Custom.

4. Type your custom format in the Type box and click OK.

When entering your format, use the following codes:

Displays the number, unless it's an insignificant zero

0 Adds zeros where needed to fill out the number

? Adds spaces where needed to align decimal points

Table 17.2 shows some sample formats.

TABLE 17.2   SAMPLE CUSTOM FORMATS

VALUE ENTERED	CUSTOM FORMAT	VALUE DISPLAYED IN CELL
3124.789	####.##	3124.79
120.5	###.#00	120.500
.6345	0.##	0.63
21456.25	##,###.00	21,456.25
120.54	$##,###.#0	$120.54

You can enter formats for how you want positive and negative numbers displayed, along with zero values and text. Simply separate the formats with a semicolon (;) like this:

##.#0;[MAGENTA] –##.#0;[GREEN] 0.00;@

In this example format, positive numbers entered into the cell are displayed with two decimal places (a zero is added to fill two decimal places if needed). Negative numbers are displayed with a preceding minus sign (–) in magenta. Zero values are displayed as 0.00 in green. Text is permitted in these cells, as indicated by the final format (@). If you do not include the text format, text you type into the cell will not be displayed at all. If you want to add a particular word or words in front of all text entered into a cell, include the word(s) in double quotation marks, as in "Acct. Code:"@.

In this lesson, you learned how to format numbers and create custom formats. In the next lesson, you will learn how to format text.

18 LESSON

GIVING YOUR TEXT A NEW LOOK

In this lesson, you learn how to change the appearance of the text in the cells.

HOW YOU CAN MAKE TEXT LOOK DIFFERENT

When you type text or numbers, Excel automatically formats it in the Arial font, which doesn't look very fancy. You can change the following text attributes to improve the appearance of your text or set it apart from other text:

Font A typeface—for example, Arial, Courier, or Times New Roman.

Font Style For example, Bold, Italic, Underline, or Strikethrough.

Text Underline versus Cell Border You can add underlining to important information in one of two ways. With the underline format explained in this lesson, a line (or lines, depending on which underline format you choose) is placed under the cell's contents. This is different from adding a line to the bottom of a cell's border, which is explained in the next lesson.

Size For example, 10-point, 12-point, or 20-point. (The higher the point size, the bigger the text is. There are approximately 72 points in an inch.)

Color   For example, Red, Magenta, or Cyan.

Alignment   For example, centered, left-aligned, or right-aligned within the cell.

 What's a Font?   A font is a set of characters that have the same typeface, which means they are of a single design (such as Times New Roman). When you select a font, you can also change the font's size; add optional *attributes* to the font, such as bold or italic; underline the text; change its color; and add special effects such as strikethrough, superscript, subscript, and small caps.

Figure 18.1 shows a worksheet after some attributes have been changed for selected text.

Row headings are set in italics.   This text is centered across columns and set in 16-point bold type.   Underline is applied to column headings.

	First Qtr	Second Qtr	Third Qtr	Fourth Qtr
Milk Pitcher	$ 4,000	$ 4,520	$ 4,120	$ 4,200
Gold Rings	$ 4,152	$ 4,692	$ 4,277	$ 4,360
Fake Ace	$ 2,513	$ 2,840	$ 2,588	$ 2,639
Sticky Cards	$ 8,754	$ 9,892	$ 9,017	$ 9,192
Magic Wand	$ 6,541	$ 7,391	$ 6,737	$ 6,868
Magic Hat	$ 4,378	$ 4,947	$ 4,509	$ 4,597

FIGURE 18.1   A sampling of several text attributes.

USING THE FORMAT CELLS DIALOG BOX

You can change the look of your text by using the Format Cells dialog box. Just follow these steps:

1. Select the cell or range that contains the text you want to format.

2. Open the Format menu and choose Cells, or press Ctrl+1. (You can also right-click the selected cells and choose Format Cells from the shortcut menu.)

3. Click the Font tab. The Font options jump to the front, as shown in Figure 18.2.

4. Select the options you want.

5. Click OK or press Enter.

Excel uses a default font to style your text as you type it. To change the default font, enter your font preferences in the Font tab and click the Normal Font option. When you click the OK button, Excel makes your preferences the default font.

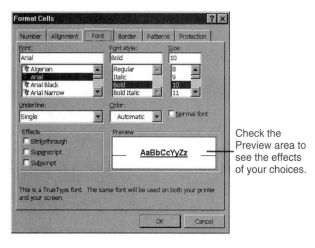

Check the Preview area to see the effects of your choices.

FIGURE 18.2   The Format Cells dialog box with the Font tab up front.

Font Shortcuts You can apply certain attributes quickly by using keyboard shortcuts. First select the cell(s), and then press Ctrl+B for bold, Ctrl+I for Italic, Ctrl+U for Single Underline (Accounting style), or Ctrl+5 for Strikethrough.

CHANGING TEXT ATTRIBUTES WITH TOOLBAR BUTTONS

A faster way to enter font changes is to use the Formatting toolbar shown in Figure 18.3.

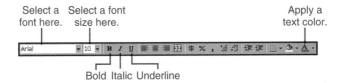

FIGURE 18.3   Use the Formatting toolbar to quickly make font changes.

To use a tool to change text attributes, follow these steps:

1. Select the cell or range that contains the text whose look you want to change.

2. To change the font or font size, pull down the appropriate drop-down list and click the font or size you want. You can also type the point size in the Font Size box.

3. To add an attribute (such as bold or underlining), click the desired button. When selected, a button looks like it has been pressed in. You can add more than one attribute to text, making it bold and italic, for example.

Change Before You Type   You can activate the attributes you want *before* you type text. For example, if you want a title in Bold 12-point Desdemona type, select the cells for which you want to change the attributes, and then set the attributes before you start typing. Unlike in a word processor where you must turn attributes on and off, in Excel, selecting formats for cells in advance of typing your data has no effect on the unselected cells; data in unselected cells will be the default Arial 10-point type.

ALIGNING TEXT IN CELLS

When you enter data into an Excel worksheet, that data is aligned automatically. Text is aligned on the left, and numbers are aligned on the right. Both text and numbers are initially set at the bottom of the cells. However, you can change both the vertical and the horizontal alignment of data in your cells.

Follow these steps to change the alignment:

1. Select the cell or range you want to align. If you want to center a title or other text over a range of cells, select the entire range of blank cells in which you want the text centered, including the cell that contains the text you want to center.

2. Pull down the Format menu and select Cells, or press Ctrl+1. The Format Cells dialog box appears.

3. Click the Alignment tab. The alignment options appear in front (see Figure 18.4).

4. Choose from the following options and option groups to set the alignment:

    Horizontal lets you specify a left/right alignment in the cell(s). (The Center Across selection centers a title or other text within a range of cells.)

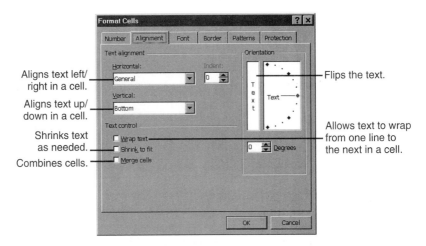

FIGURE 18.4   The Alignment options.

Vertical lets you specify how you want the text aligned in relation to the top and bottom of the cell(s).

Orientation lets you flip the text sideways or print it from top to bottom (instead of left to right). This option is new to Excel 97.

Wrap Text tells Excel to wrap long lines of text within a cell without changing the width of cell. (Normally, Excel displays all text in a cell on one line.)

Shrink to Fit shrinks the text to fit within the cell's current width. If the cell's width is adjusted, the text increases or decreases in size accordingly.

Merge Cells combines several cells into a single cell. All data is overlaid, except for the cell in the upper-left corner of the selected cells.

5. Click OK or press Enter.

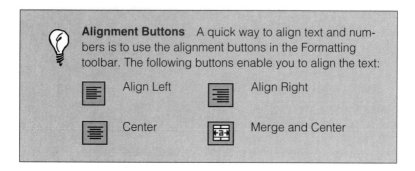

Alignment Buttons   A quick way to align text and numbers is to use the alignment buttons in the Formatting toolbar. The following buttons enable you to align the text:

Align Left   Align Right

Center   Merge and Center

New to Excel 97 is the capability to indent your text within a cell. If you're typing a paragraph worth of information into a single cell, you can indent that paragraph by selecting left alignment from the Horizontal list box in the Format Cells dialog box (as explained earlier). After selecting left alignment, set the amount of indent you want with the Indent spin box.

In addition, you can add an indent quickly by clicking the following buttons on the Formatting toolbar:

 Decrease Indent   Removes an indent or creates a negative indent.

 Increase Indent   Adds an indent.

In this lesson, you learned how to customize your text formatting to achieve the look you want. In the next lesson, you will learn how to add borders and shading to your worksheet.

ADDING CELL BORDERS AND SHADING

In this lesson, you will learn how to add pizzazz to your worksheets by adding borders and shading.

ADDING BORDERS TO CELLS

As you work with your worksheet on-screen, you'll notice that each cell is identified by gridlines that surround the cell. Normally, these gridlines do not print; and even if you choose to print them, they may appear washed out. To have more well-defined lines appear on the printout (or on-screen, for that matter), you can add borders to selected cells or entire cell ranges. A border can appear on all four sides of a cell or only on selected sides, whichever you prefer.

 The Gridlines Don't Print? In Excel 97, as in Excel 95, the gridlines do not print by default. But if you want to try printing your worksheet with gridlines first just to see what it looks like, open the File menu, select Page Setup, click the Sheet tab, select Gridlines, and click OK.

To add borders to a cell or range, perform the following steps:

1. Select the cell(s) around which you want a border to appear.

2. Open the Format menu and choose Cells. The Format Cells dialog box appears.

3. Click the Border tab to see the Border options shown in Figure 19.1.

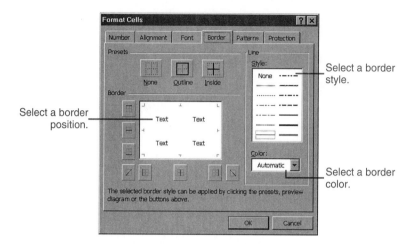

Select a border style.

Select a border position.

Select a border color.

Figure 19.1   Choose border options from the Format Cells dialog box.

4. Select the desired position, style (thickness), and color for the border. You can click inside the Border box itself, or you can click a preset border pattern button to add your border.

5. Click OK or press Enter.

Hiding Gridlines   When adding borders to a worksheet, you might need to hide the gridlines to get a better idea of how the borders will look when printed. Open the Tools menu, select Options, click the View tab, and select Gridlines to remove the check mark from the check box. Of course, selecting this option has no effect on whether or not the gridlines actually print, only on whether or not they are displayed on-screen.

To add borders quickly, select the cells around which you want the border to appear, and then click the Borders drop-down arrow in the Formatting toolbar. Click the desired border. If you click the Borders button itself (instead of the arrow), Excel automatically adds the border line you last chose to the selected cells.

ADDING SHADING TO CELLS

For a simple but dramatic effect, you can add shading to your worksheets. With shading, you can add a color or gray shading to a cell. You can add colors at full strength or partial strength to create the exact effect you want. To lessen the strength of the cell color you select, you add your shading with a pattern, such as a diagonal. Figure 19.2 illustrates some of the effects you can create with shading.

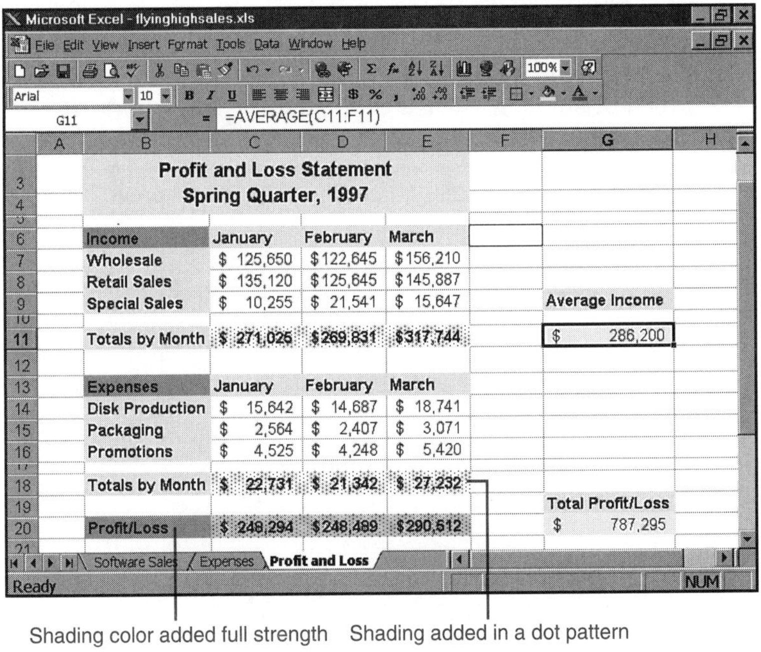

Shading color added full strength   Shading added in a dot pattern

FIGURE 19.2   A worksheet with added shading.

Follow these steps to add shading to a cell or range. As you make your selections, keep in mind that if you plan to print your worksheet with a black and white printer, your pretty colors may not be different enough to create the effect you want. Select colors that contrast well in value (intensity), and use the Print Preview command (as explained in Lesson 11) to view your results in black and white before you print.

1. Select the cell(s) you want to shade.

2. Open the Format menu and choose Cells.

3. Click the Patterns tab. Excel displays the shading options (see Figure 19.3).

4. Click the Pattern drop-down arrow, and you will see a grid that contains all the colors from the color palette, as well as patterns. Select the shading color and pattern you want to use. The Color options let you choose a color for the overall shading. The Pattern options let you select a black-and-white or colored pattern that lies on top of the overall shading. A preview of the result appears in the Sample box.

5. When you like the results you see, click OK or press Enter.

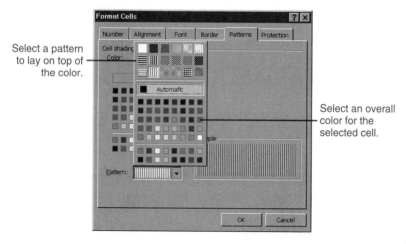

Select a pattern to lay on top of the color.

Select an overall color for the selected cell.

Figure 19.3　Selecting a shading and a pattern.

A quick way to add cell shading (without a pattern) is to select the cells you want to shade, click the Fill Color drop-down arrow, and click the color you want to use.

> **Quick Color** To add the color shown in the bucket of the Fill Color button, simply click the button itself—do not bother to click the arrow to the right of the button.

If the shading is too dark, consider using the Font Color button (just to the right of the Fill Color button) to select a lighter color for the text.

USING AUTOFORMAT

Excel offers the AutoFormat feature, which takes some of the pain out of formatting. AutoFormat provides you with 16 predesigned table formats that you can apply to a worksheet.

To use predesigned formats, perform the following steps:

1. Select the worksheet(s) and cell(s) that contain the data you want to format.

2. Open the Format menu and choose AutoFormat. The AutoFormat dialog box appears, as shown in Figure 19.4.

3. In the Table Format list, choose the predesigned format you want to use. When you select a format, Excel shows you what it will look like in the Sample area.

4. To exclude certain elements from AutoFormat, click the Options button and choose the formats you want to turn off.

5. Click OK, and Excel formats your table to make it look like the one in the preview area.

> **Unformatting an AutoFormat** If you don't like what AutoFormat did to your worksheet, select the table, open the Format menu, and choose AutoFormat. From the Table format list, choose None to remove the AutoFormat.

Select a predesigned table format.

Format options that you can turn off (these options appear after you click the Options button).

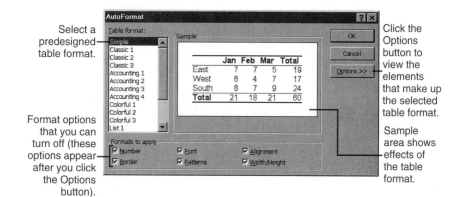

Click the Options button to view the elements that make up the selected table format.

Sample area shows effects of the table format.

FIGURE 19.4   Use the AutoFormat dialog box to select a prefab format.

COPYING FORMATS WITH FORMAT PAINTER

Excel gives you two ways to copy and paste formatting:

- You can use the Edit, Copy command and then the Edit Paste Special command and select Formats from the Paste options in the Paste Special dialog box.

- You can use the Format Painter button in the Standard toolbar.

The Format Painter lets you quickly copy and paste formats that you have already used in a workbook. Because the Format Painter button is faster, I'll give you the steps you need to paint formats.

1. Select the cell(s) that contain the formatting you want to copy and paste.

2. Click the Format Painter button on the Standard toolbar. Excel copies the formatting. The mouse pointer changes into a paintbrush with a plus sign next to it.

3. Click and drag over the cells to which you want to apply the copied formatting.

4. Release the mouse button, and Excel copies the formatting and applies it to the selected cells.

 Faster Painter   To paint several areas at one time, double-click the Format Painter button. Then drag over the first section you want to paint. The cursor remains as a paintbrush, meaning that you can continue to drag over other cells to paint them too. When you're through, press Esc to return to a normal cursor.

APPLYING CONDITIONAL FORMATTING

If you want to highlight particular values in your worksheet, you can use conditional formatting. For example, if you want to highlight all sales figures under a particular mark, you could apply a conditional red shading.

To apply conditional formatting, follow these steps:

1. Select the cells you want to format.

2. Open the Format menu and select Conditional Formatting. The Conditional Formatting dialog box appears, as shown in Figure 19.5.

3. To apply a format based on the value found in a selected cell, choose Cell Value Is from the Condition 1 list.

   To apply a format based on the value found in a cell outside the selected range, select Formula Is from the Condition 1 list.

4. Enter the value or formula you want to use as the *condition* that determines when Excel can apply the formatting you select. If you choose to use a formula, be sure to include the beginning equal (=) sign.

FIGURE 19.5   Apply formats conditionally to highlight certain values.

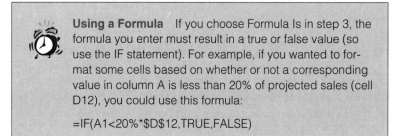

Using a Formula   If you choose Formula Is in step 3, the formula you enter must result in a true or false value (so use the IF statement). For example, if you wanted to format some cells based on whether or not a corresponding value in column A is less than 20% of projected sales (cell D12), you could use this formula:

=IF(A1<20%*D12,TRUE,FALSE)

5. Click the Format button and select the format you want to apply when the condition is true. Click OK to return to the Conditional Formatting dialog box.

6. (Optional) If you want to add more than one condition, click Add. Then repeat steps 3 and 4 to add the condition.

7. When you finish adding conditions, click OK.

You can copy the conditional formatting from one cell to other cells using the Format Painter button. Simply click the cell whose formatting you want to copy and click the Format Painter button. Then drag over the cells to which you want to copy the formatting.

In this lesson, you learned some ways to enhance the appearance of your worksheets. In the next lesson, you will learn how to change the sizes of rows and columns.

CHANGING COLUMN WIDTH AND ROW HEIGHT

In this lesson, you will learn how to adjust the column width and row height to make the best use of the worksheet space. You can set these manually or let Excel make the adjustments for you with its AutoFit feature.

ADJUSTING COLUMN WIDTH AND ROW HEIGHT WITH A MOUSE

You can adjust the width of a column or the height of a row by using a dialog box or by dragging with the mouse.

Why Bother? You might not want to bother adjusting the row height because it's automatically adjusted as you change font size. However, if a column's width is not as large as it's data, that data might not be displayed and might appear as **########**. In such a case, you must adjust the width of the column in order for the data to be displayed at all.

Here's how you adjust the row height or column width with the mouse:

1. To change the row height or column width of a single row or column, skip to step 2. To change the height or width of two or more rows or columns, select them first by dragging over the row or column headings.

2. Position the mouse pointer over one of the row heading or column heading borders as shown in Figure 20.1. (Use the right border of the column heading to adjust column width; use the bottom border of the row heading to adjust the row height.)

3. Drag the border to the size you need it to be.

4. Release the mouse button, and Excel adjusts the row height or column width.

Dragging the right border of column A changes its width.

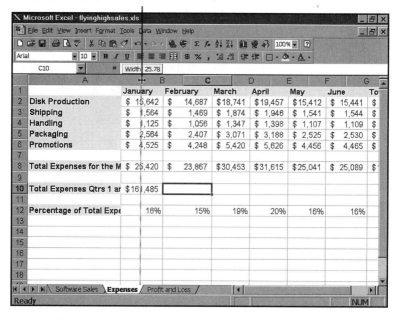

Figure 20.1 The mouse pointer changes to a double-headed arrow when you move it over a border in the row or column heading.

AutoFit Cells   To quickly make a column as wide as its widest entry using Excel's AutoFit feature, double-click the right border of the column heading. To make a row as tall as its tallest entry, double-click on the bottom border of the row heading. To change more than one column or row at a time, drag over the desired row or column headings, and then double-click the bottommost or rightmost heading border.

USING THE FORMAT MENU FOR PRECISE CONTROL

You can change a row or column's size by dragging the border of a row or column. However, you cannot control the size as precisely as you can by providing specific sizes with the Format, Row Height and Format, Column Width commands.

These steps show you how to use the Format menu to change the column width:

1. Select the column(s) whose width you want to change. To change the width of a single column, select any cell in that column.

2. Open the Format menu, select Column, and select Width. The Column Width dialog box appears (see Figure 20.2).

3. Type the number of characters you would like as the width. The default width is 8.43.

4. Click OK or press Enter to put your changes into effect.

FIGURE 20.2   Changing the column width.

By default, Excel makes a row a bit taller than the tallest text in the row. For example, if the tallest text is 10 points tall, Excel makes the row itself 12.75 points tall. You can use the Format menu to change the row height manually:

1. Select the row(s) whose height you want to change. (To change the height of a single row, select any cell in that row.)

2. Open the Format menu, select Row, and select Height. The Row Height dialog box shown in Figure 20.3 appears.

3. Type the desired height (in points).

4. Click OK or press Enter to implement the change in your worksheet.

FIGURE 20.3   Changing the row height.

In this lesson, you learned how to change the row height and column width. In the next lesson, you will learn how to use Excel with the Internet.

EXCEL AND THE INTERNET

21

In this lesson, you will learn how to prepare worksheets for use on the Internet.

SAVING A WORKSHEET IN HTML FORMAT

You can publish your Excel data on a Web site (or on your company's intranet) by converting your workbook to *HTML format*. Note, however, that PivotTables, AutoFilters, number formats, and formulas might not be converted properly, so you might have to do some tweaking to the completed HTML document.

HTML   Short for HyperText Markup Language, HTML is the language in which data is presented on the World Wide Web. To display your Excel data on the Web, you must convert it to this format.

Once you've prepared your data, you can save it in HTML by following these steps:

1. Select the first range of data you want to convert to HTML.

2. Open the File menu and select Save As HTML. The Internet Assistant Wizard — Step 1 of 4 dialog box appears.

Missing Your Assistant?   If Internet Assistant was not installed when you installed Microsoft Excel, open the Tools menu and select Add-Ins. Select Internet Assistant Wizard from the Add-ins Available list and click OK.

3. The data range you selected in step 1 appears in the text box. If you want to add more data ranges to the selection (such as data on a different worksheet), click Add, select the range, and then click OK. When you're through, click Next>.

4. Select either Create an Independent, Ready-to-View HTML Document or Insert the Converted Data into an Existing HTML File. Then click Next>.

5. If you're creating a new HTML document, make selections for the header and footer information, as shown in Figure 21.1, and click Next>. If you're inserting data into an existing HTML file, you'll see a different screen. Skip to step 8.

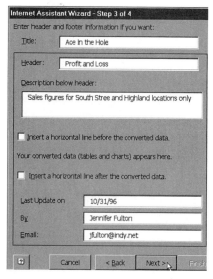

FIGURE 21.1   Select your header and footer information.

6. Choose whether to Save the Result As an HTML File or Add the Result to My FrontPage Web. Enter the file name you want to use in the File Path text box, or click Browse and select a directory from the resulting dialog box.

What's a FrontPage Web?   FrontPage is Microsoft's HTML editor; when you use it to create a Web site, it stores the data on your hard disk temporarily. If you use FrontPage, you can add your converted Excel data to your Web directory if you want.

7. Click Finish, and the selected data is converted to HTML format.

8. If you selected Insert the Converted Data into an Existing HTML File in step 4, the resulting screen looks like the one shown in Figure 21.2. Open the HTML file in which you want your Excel data placed (using an HTML editor) and add the following text, which acts as a marker, telling Excel where to place the table in the file.

    <!--##Table##-->

Then save the file in the HTML Editor. Type the path to your HTML file in the Path of the Existing File text box, or click Browse and locate it manually. When you're done, click Next>.

Let FrontPage Do It for You   If you use FrontPage, select the Open the File from My FrontPage Web option, and the Internet Assistant Wizard will open FrontPage for you so you can add the ##Table## marker.

9. Select a new code page if necessary, and then choose how you want the Internet Assistant Wizard to save your file (see Figure 21.3). If you want to save the result as a new file, type a name in the File Path text box. If you want the IAW to replace your existing HTML file, type its name instead or click Browse to select it.

10. When you're done, click Finish, and the selected table is added to the specified HTML file. To view the table in your favorite browser, select File, Open File.

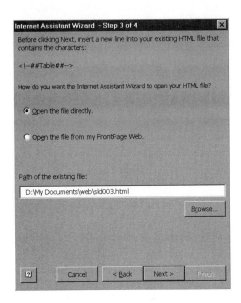

FIGURE 21.2   Open your existing HTML file.

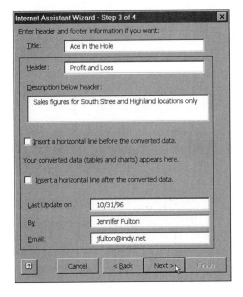

FIGURE 21.3   Choose how you want to save your table.

ADDING HYPERLINKS TO A WORKSHEET

A hyperlink is a bit of text or a graphic that, when clicked, takes the user to a Web page, to a file on your hard disk, or to a file on a local network. To add a hyperlink to a worksheet, follow these steps:

1. Select the cell(s) that contain the text you want to use for the link. For example, the cell might contain the text **Click here to view supporting statistics**. If you do not enter any text, Excel will insert the address of the file you select in step 4. If you want to use a graphic or a drawing as a link, select it instead.

2. Click the Insert Hyperlink button on the Standard toolbar.

3. If asked, make sure you save your workbook. The Insert Hyperlink dialog box appears, as shown in Figure 21.4.

Type an address.

Type an anchor if you want.

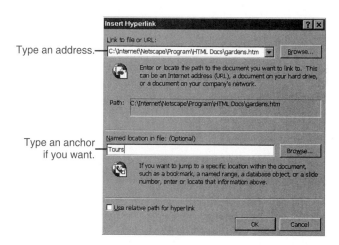

FIGURE 21.4   Insert a hyperlink in a workbook.

4. Type the address of the Web page or file to which you want to link in the Link to File or URL text box, or click Browse to select it from a dialog box.

5. If you want to jump to a particular location within your file, enter that location in the Named Location in File text box. If the destination file is an Excel file, you can enter a named range, a sheet, or cell address. In an HTML file, you can enter the name of an anchor.

6. Click Use Relative Path for Hyperlink if you want Excel to use the destination file's relative address, rather than its actual address. A relative address can be easily changed if you think that the file to which the link refers will be moved.

Changing a Relative Address   To change a relative address, change the base address to which the address relates. For example, if the link points to an Excel file on your hard disk, and you always saved your workbooks in the directory C:\MYDOCS, but now you've moved them to the F:\PUBLIC\EXCEL\, open the File menu, select Properties, enter the new base address in the Hyperlink Base text box, and click OK.

7. Click OK. The text in the cell you selected becomes blue and underlined.

When you move the mouse pointer over this link, it changes to a hand. Next to the hand, you can see the address of the destination file. Click the link, and the destination file opens. (Of course, if the link points to a file on the Internet, you need to connect to the Internet first and then click the link.)

If you need to change the text for a link later on, click a cell next to the link, and then use the arrow keys to move the pointer to the link cell. You can then change the text for the link by changing it in the Formula bar. To select a graphic link, press and hold Ctrl and click the graphic. Then use the Drawing or Picture toolbar to change it.

You can also change the destination of the link by following these steps to select the link and then clicking the Insert Hyperlink button.

If you need to delete the link, select it and press Delete. To move the link, select it and use the Edit, Cut and Edit, Paste commands to move it to a new cell.

In this lesson, you learned how to use Excel with the Internet. In the next lesson, you'll learn how to create charts from your Excel data.

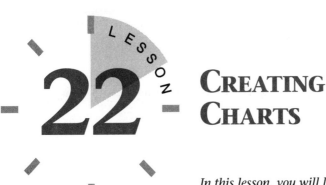

22

CREATING CHARTS

In this lesson, you will learn to create charts to represent your workbook data as a picture.

CHART TYPES

With Excel, you can create various types of charts. Some common chart types are shown in Figure 22.1. The chart type you choose depends on your data and on how you want to present that data. These are the major chart types and their purposes:

Pie Use this chart to show the relationship among parts of a whole.

Bar Use this chart to compare values at a given point in time.

Column Similar to the Bar chart; use this chart to emphasize the difference between items.

Line Use this chart to emphasize trends and the change of values over time.

Scatter Similar to a Line chart; use this chart to emphasize the difference between two sets of values.

Area Similar to the Line chart; use this chart to emphasize the amount of change in values over time.

Most of these basic chart types also come in three-dimensional varieties. In addition to looking more professional than the standard flat charts, 3-D charts can often help your audience distinguish between different sets of data.

Area chart   Bar chart   Pie chart   Column chart   Line chart

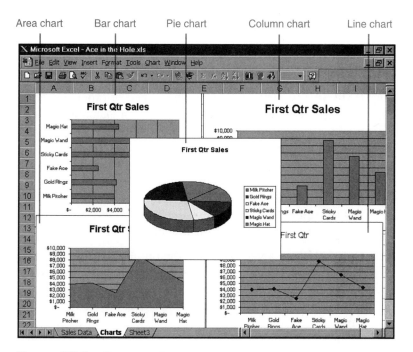

FIGURE 22.1   Common Excel chart types.

 Embedded Charts   A chart that is placed on the same worksheet that contains the data used to create the chart. A chart can also be placed on a chart sheet in the workbook so that the worksheet and chart are separate. Embedded charts are useful for showing the actual data and its graphic representation side-by-side.

 Upgrade Tip   Excel 97 includes many new chart types, so have fun when selecting the one you want to use.

CHARTING TERMINOLOGY

Before you start creating charts, familiarize yourself with the following terminology:

Data Series   The bars, pie wedges, lines, or other elements that represent plotted values in a chart. For example, a chart might show a set of similar bars that reflects a series of values for the same item. The bars in the series would all have the same pattern. If you have more than one pattern of bars, each pattern would represent a separate data series. For instance, charting the sales for Territory 1 versus Territory 2 would require two data series—one for each territory. Often, data series correspond to rows of data in your worksheet.

Categories   Categories reflect the number of elements in a series. You might have two data series to compare the sales of two different territories and four categories to compare these sales over four quarters. Some charts have only one category, and others have several. Categories normally correspond to the columns that you have in your chart data and the category labels coming from the column headings.

Axis   One side of a chart. A two-dimensional chart has an x-axis (horizontal) and a y-axis (vertical). The x-axis contains all the data series and categories in the chart. If you have more than one category, the x-axis often contains labels that define what each category represents. The y-axis reflects the values of the bars, lines, or plot points. In a three-dimensional chart, the z-axis represents the vertical plane, and the x-axis (distance) and y-axis (width) represent the two sides on the floor of the chart.

Legend   Defines the separate series of a chart. For example, the legend for a pie chart will show what each piece of the pie represents.

Gridlines   Emphasize the y-axis or x-axis scale of the data series. For example, major gridlines for the y-axis will help you follow a point from the x- or y-axis to identify a data point's exact value.

CREATING A CHART

You can create charts as part of a worksheet (an embedded chart) or as a chart on a separate worksheet. If you create an embedded chart, it will print side-by-side with your worksheet data. If you create a chart on a separate worksheet, you can print it independently. Both types of charts are linked to the worksheet data that they represent, so when you change the data, the chart is automatically updated.

The Chart Wizard button in the Standard toolbar enables you to quickly create a chart. To use the Chart Wizard, follow these steps:

1. Select the data you want to chart. If you typed names or other labels (such as Qtr 1, Qtr 2, and so on) and you want them included in the chart, make sure you select them.

 2. Click the Chart Wizard button on the Standard toolbar.

3. The Chart Wizard Step 1 of 4 dialog box appears, as shown in Figure 22.2. Select a Chart Type and select a Chart Sub-Type (a variation on the selected chart type). Click Next>.

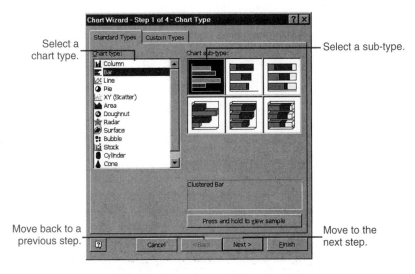

FIGURE 22.2 Chart Wizard asks you to choose the chart type.

4. Next you're asked if the selected range is correct. You can correct the range by typing a new range or by clicking the Collapse Dialog button (located at the right end of the Data Range text box) and selecting the range you want to use.

5. By default, Excel assumes that your different data series are stored in rows. You can change this to columns if necessary by clicking the Series in Columns option. When you're through, click Next>.

6. Click the various tabs to change options for your chart (see Figure 22.3). For example, you can delete the legend by clicking the Legend tab and deselecting Show Legend. You can add a chart title on the Titles tab. Add data labels (labels which display the actual value being represented by each bar, line, and so on) by clicking the Data Labels tab. When you finish making changes, click Next.

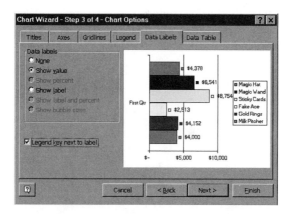

FIGURE 22.3   Select from various chart appearance options.

7. Finally, you're asked if you want to embed the chart (as an object) in the current worksheet, or if you want to create a new worksheet for it. Make your selection and click the Finish button. Your completed chart appears.

Moving and Resizing a Chart   To move an embedded chart, click anywhere in the chart area and drag it to the new location. To change the size of a chart, select the chart, and then drag one of its *handles* (the black squares that border the chart). Drag a corner handle to change the height and width, or drag a side handle to change only the width. (Note that you can't really resize a chart that is on a sheet by itself.)

Create a Chart Fast!   To create a chart quickly, select the data you want to use and press F11. Excel creates a column chart (the default chart type) on its own sheet. You can switch to that sheet, select the chart, and customize it as needed.

CUSTOMIZING YOUR CHART WITH THE CHART TOOLBAR

You can use the Chart toolbar to change how your chart looks. If the Chart toolbar is not displayed, you can turn it on by opening the View menu, selecting Toolbars, and then selecting Chart.

Table 22.1 shows each button on the Chart toolbar and explains its purpose.

TABLE 22.1   BUTTONS ON THE CHART TOOLBAR

BUTTON	NAME	USE
[_____▼]	Chart Objects	Click here to select the part of the chart you want to change. Or, you can simply click the part itself.

continues

TABLE 22.1   CONTINUED

BUTTON	NAME	USE
	Format Object	Click here to change the formatting of the object whose name appears in the Chart Objects text box.
	Chart Type	Click the arrow to change the chart type, from bar to line, for example. If you click the button itself, the displayed chart type will be applied.
	Legend	Click this to display or hide the legend.
	Data Table	Click here to add a data table (a grid which displays the data from which the chart was created).
	By Row	Click here if your data series are stored in rows.
	By Column	Click here if your data series are stored in columns.
	Angle Text Downward	Click here to angle text in selected area downward.
	Angle Text Upward	Click here to angle text in selected area upward.

For help customizing your chart, see the next lesson.

SAVING CHARTS

The charts you create are part of the current workbook. To save a chart, simply save the workbook that contains the chart. For more details, refer to Lesson 7, "Creating and Saving Workbook Files."

PRINTING A CHART

If a chart is an embedded chart, it will print when you print the worksheet that contains the chart. If you want to print just the embedded chart, click it to select it, and then open the File menu and select Print. Make sure that the Selected Chart option is turned on. Then click OK to print the chart.

If you created a chart on a separate worksheet, you can print the chart separately by printing only that worksheet. For more information about printing, refer to Lesson 11, "Printing Your Workbook."

In this lesson, you learned about the different chart types and how to create them. You also learned how to save and print charts. In the next lesson, you will learn how to enhance your charts.

Enhancing Charts

In this lesson, you will learn how to enhance your charts to display data more clearly and attractively.

Selecting a Chart Part

A chart is made up of several independent objects. For example, a chart may have a title, a legend, and various data series. Before you can add enhancements to a chart, you must first select the part of the chart you want to change. To do that, simply click that part or select it from the Chart Objects box on the Chart toolbar. (To display the Chart toolbar, open the View menu, select Toolbars, and select Chart.) When a part is selected, *handles* (tiny black squares) form a box around it, as shown in Figure 23.1.

Upgrade Tip   Whereas in previous versions of Excel you had to double-click the chart to edit it, in Excel 97, you click only once.

When a part is selected, you can move it by dragging it wherever you want and releasing the mouse button. To resize a part, select it and then drag one of its handles outward to make the object larger or inward to make it smaller. When the object is the size you want it, release the mouse button. You can resize the whole chart by selecting it first and then dragging one of its handles.

The following sections tell you how to make some common enhancements to a chart.

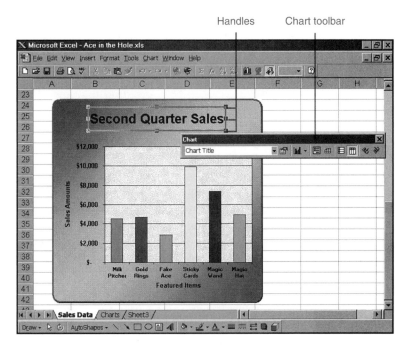

FIGURE 23.1   When a part is selected, it's surrounded by handles.

CHANGING THE CHART TYPE

To change the type of chart from a line chart to a pie chart, for example, follow these steps:

1. Click the chart to select it, or choose Chart Area from the Chart Objects drop-down list on the Chart toolbar. Handles appear around the whole chart.

2. Click the Chart Type button to change the chart to the displayed type, or click the drop-down arrow and select another type.

> **The Type I Want Isn't Displayed!**   To change to a chart
> type that is not on the list, open the Chart menu and se-
> lect Chart Type. You can choose from a number of cus-
> tom chart types in this dialog box.

ADDING A TITLE AND A LEGEND

You can add various titles to a chart to help indicate what the
chart is all about. You can add a chart title that appears at the top
of the chart, and you can add axis titles that appear along the
x- and y-axes (and the z-axis as well, if the chart is a 3-D chart).
You can also add a *legend*—a small table that describes what each
element in the chart represents.

Here's how you do it:

1. Click the chart to select it, or choose Chart Area from
   the Chart Objects drop-down list on the Chart toolbar.
   Handles appear around the whole chart.

2. Open the Chart menu and select Chart Options. The
   Chart Options dialog appears, as shown in Figure 23.2.

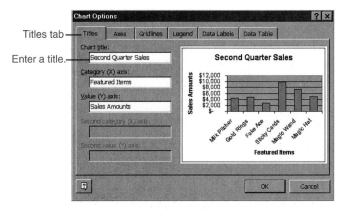

FIGURE **23.2**   Add additional titles to your chart.

3. Click the Titles tab, and then add the titles you want. A sample chart appears on the right so you can see what your changes will look like.

4. To add a legend, click the Legend tab. Click the Show Legend option if needed to turn it on. Then select where you want the legend placed.

5. When you finish, click OK.

 More Text If you want to add text that is not a chart title or axis title, click the Drawing button on the Standard toolbar to display the Drawing toolbar. Click the Text Box button (the button in the Drawing toolbar with a piece of paper and horizontal lines), and then drag the mouse pointer to create the text box. When you release the mouse button, an insertion point appears inside the text box. Type your text. You can use this same technique to add text to your worksheets as well.

FORMATTING TEXT AND NUMBERS

All the text on a chart appears inside its own text box. To format text or numbers on a chart, follow these steps:

1. Click the text you want to change, or select it from the Chart Objects drop-down list on the Chart toolbar. To change the text for the entire chart, select Chart Area.

 2. Click the Format Object button on the Chart toolbar. The dialog box that appears differs slightly from object to object, but no matter.

3. Click the Font tab. The Font options enable you to change the font, style, size, and color of the text (see Figure 23.3).

4. To change the text's alignment, click the Alignment tab. You can choose to display the text at an angle to save room, if necessary.

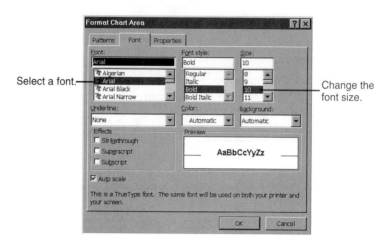

Select a font.

Change the font size.

FIGURE 23.3 Change the look of text with options on the Font tab.

5. To change the way numbers look, click the Number tab. Then select a Category and choose from the other available options shown in Figure 23.4.

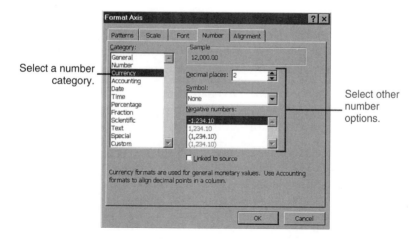

Select a number category.

Select other number options.

FIGURE 23.4 Change the look of numbers on the Number tab.

6. Click OK when you are finished.

ENHANCING THE CHART AREA

One way to make your chart stand out is to change its frame (the box in which the chart appears). You can also change the background that fills the frame. In addition, you can enhance the plot area (the area in which the data appears) by adding a colorful border or changing its color or pattern.

To enhance the chart area, follow these steps:

1. Click the object you want to change, or select it from the Chart Objects drop-down list on the Chart toolbar. To change the chart's background or border, select Chart Area. To change the plot background or border, select Plot Area instead.

2. Click the Format Object button on the Chart toolbar.

3. Click the Patterns tab, and you'll see the options shown in Figure 23.5.

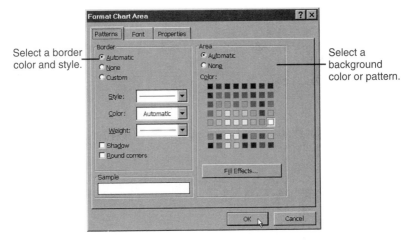

Select a border color and style.

Select a background color or pattern.

FIGURE 23.5   Change the background and border of your chart with the Patterns tab.

4. To change the border of the selected area, choose from the options in the Border section. You can change the style, color, and weight (thickness) of the border. Your selections appear in the Sample area so you can see how they'll look.

5. To change the background of the selected area, choose from the options in the Area section. Here, you can select a color for the background. If you click Fill Effects, you can choose from various gradient fills, textures, and patterns. You can even use a graphic as the background for your chart if you want.

6. When you're through, click OK.

In this lesson, you learned how to improve the appearance of your chart. In the next lesson, you will learn other ways in which you can customize your chart.

More Ways to Enhance Charts

In this lesson, you will learn how to customize and modify your charts with some of Excel's powerful charting capabilities.

Changing the Gridlines

By default, horizontal gridlines appear in an Excel chart. You can change to vertical gridlines only or a combination of both horizontal and vertical. In addition, you can change the value gridline's upper and lower limits and the interval between major gridlines. Also, you can display minor gridlines.

 Major and Minor Gridlines Major gridlines help you pinpoint exact locations in a chart without cluttering the chart. When major gridlines don't provide enough detail, you can use minor gridlines as well. Minor gridlines fall between the major intervals on the axis.

Changing the Gridline Display

To change to vertical gridlines (or a combination of horizontal and vertical) or to display minor gridlines, this is what you do:

1. Click the chart. Then open the Chart menu and select Chart Options. The Chart Options dialog box appears.

2. Click the Gridlines tab.

3. Select the gridlines you want to display. Your selections appear in the sample area so you can see how they'll look.

4. Click OK.

CHANGING THE START AND STOP VALUES

You can change the start and stop value used on the value axis (the axis against which the values are plotted—typically, the y-axis), or you can change the interval between gridlines. You might need to do this, for example, to shorten the value axis in order to draw attention to the difference between two data series. Follow these steps:

1. Select Value Axis from the Chart Objects drop-down list on the Chart toolbar.

 2. Click the Format Object button.

3. Click the Scale tab, and you'll see the options shown in Figure 24.1.

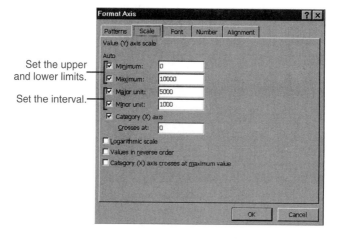

FIGURE 24.1 Change the gridline values with the Scale tab.

4. Change the minimum or maximum values used to plot the data if you want. For example, if the maximum value is 12,000 but the maximum data value is only 9,800, you might want to change the maximum value to 10,000 in order to tighten up the plot area.

5. To change the interval between gridlines, change the value under Major Unit. If you're displaying minor gridlines too, you may want to adjust that Minor Unit value as well.

6. You can adjust the point at which the x-axis crosses the y-axis by changing the value under Category (X) Axis Crosses At. If you want the x-axis to cross the y-axis at its highest value (you want to place the categories at the top of the chart), select the Category (X) Axis Crosses at Maximum Value option instead.

7. To recalculate the minimum, maximum, and interval values based on the range of data values in your chart, select the Logarithmic Scale option.

 Negative Idea If your chart contains negative values, do *not* select the Logarithmic Scale option.

8. To change the direction of the bars or columns in a chart, select the Values in Reverse Order option.

9. When you're finished, click OK.

CHANGING THE CATEGORY AXIS

You can customize the category axis (the x-axis) as well. For example, you can increase the space between columns (or bars, and so on.) To learn how, follow these steps:

1. Choose Category Axis from the Chart Objects drop-down list on the Chart toolbar.

 2. Click the Format Object button.

3. Click the Scale tab, and you'll see the options shown in Figure 24.2.

4. You can change the point at which the value axis (y-axis) crosses the category axis (x-axis) by entering a different category number in the Value (Y) Axis Crosses at Category Number box.

5. To label every other category, enter a 2 in the Number of Categories Between Tick-Mark Labels text box. To label every third category instead, enter a 3 instead, etc.

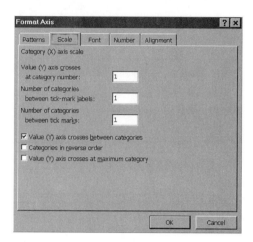

FIGURE 24.2 You can customize the Category axis as well.

6. To display more categories between the tick-marks on the x-axis, change the value under Number of Categories Between Tick-Marks.

7. If the Value (Y) Axis Crosses Between Categories option is *not* selected, then no space will appear between the first and last categories, and the edges of the plot area.

8. Reverse the order in which the categories are plotted by selecting the Categories in Reverse Order option.

9. If you want the value labels to appear on the right-hand side of the plot area instead of the left, select the Value (Y) Axis Crosses at Maximum Category option.

10. Click OK when you're through.

CHANGING THE PERSPECTIVE OF 3-D CHARTS

3-D charts are commonly used to illustrate volume. In order to make the various three-dimensional elements stand out, you may want to tilt the plot area or rotate it. Here's how you do that:

1. Choose Corners from the Chart Objects drop-down list on the Chart toolbar.

2. Click the lower-right corner, as shown in Figure 24.3.

3. Drag the corner to change the 3-D perspective of the plot area. A wire frame follows the mouse pointer to show you approximately how your chart will look in that perspective.

4. When you like the perspective, release the mouse button. Excel redraws your 3-D chart to match the perspective you choose.

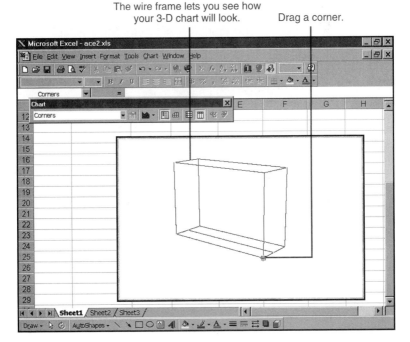

FIGURE 24.3   Changing the 3-D view.

SELECTING DATA SERIES OPTIONS

All chart types come with special options that you can select in order to emphasize certain values in your particular chart. For example, a column chart allows you to set the gap width (the width between categories) and the overlap (the amount that columns in different series overlap). In addition, if the column chart uses only a single series, by default all the columns are the same color. You can tell Excel to display them in different colors if you like. On a line chart, you can add drop lines (lines which help you view the differences between different series), change the markers, and add high-low lines. Each chart type has its own special options from which you can choose.

To select from the various data series options, follow these steps:

1. Choose Series "x" from the Chart Objects drop-down list on the Chart toolbar.

 Which Series? If your chart includes several series, select the series you want to change. However, most of the time, it doesn't matter which series you select, because the majority of these options apply to all the series in a chart, and not to a particular one.

 2. Click the Format Object button. The Format Data Series dialog box appears.

3. Click the Options tab.

4. Select from the available options. For example, on a column chart, adjust the gap width if you like.

5. Click the Patterns tab. Sometimes additional options appear here. For example, on a line chart, you can change the style of the marker from this tab. Anyway, select whatever options you desire.

6. Click OK when you're through.

Changing Data Series Values

As you fine-tune your chart, you may discover that you originally selected the wrong cells for a particular data series. Or you may want to add an additional series to a chart. Both options are easy to complete using the Source Data dialog box. Here's how:

1. Click the chart to select it.

2. Open the Chart menu and select Source Data. The Source Data dialog box opens, as shown in Figure 24.4.

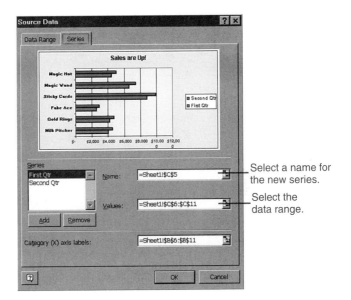

Select a name for the new series.

Select the data range.

FIGURE 24.4   Change your data series.

3. Click the Series tab.

4. To remove a series, select it from the Series list and click Remove.

5. To add a new series, click Add. Then either type the appropriate range address in the Name and Values text boxes, or click the Collapse Dialog button and select the ranges you want to use from the worksheet.

6. Repeat step 5 to add additional series. The sample chart changes to reflect your additions and deletions.

7. When you finish making changes to your data series, click OK.

In this lesson, you learned additional ways you can customize your chart. In the next lesson, you will learn how to turn your worksheet data into a database.

25

WORKING WITH A DATABASE

In this lesson, you will learn some database basics and how to create your own database.

DATABASE BASICS

A *database* is a tool used for storing, organizing, and retrieving information. For example, if you want to save the names and addresses of all the people on your holiday card list, you can create a database and then save the following information for each person: first name, last name, street number, and so on. Each piece of information is entered into a separate *field* (cell) in the list. All of the fields for one person in the list make a *record*.

In Excel, a cell is a field, and a row of field entries makes a record. The column headings in the list are called *field names* in the database. Figure 25.1 shows a database and its component parts.

Database or Data List? Excel has simplified the database operations by treating the database as a simple *list* of data. You enter the database information just like you would enter data into a worksheet. When you select a command from the Data menu, Excel recognizes the list as a database.

Each row is a record.   Field names are used   Each cell contains
as column headings.   a single field entry.

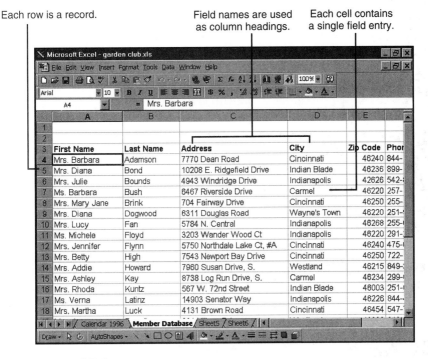

FIGURE 25.1   The parts of a database.

You must observe the following rules when you enter information
into your database:

- **Field Names**: You must enter field names in the first
  row of the database. For example, you might type **First
  Name** for the column that will hold first names, and you
  might type **Last Name** for the column that will hold last
  names. Do *not* skip a row between the field names row
  and the first record.

- **Records**: Each record must be in a separate row, and
  there cannot be any empty rows between records.

- **Same Stuff**: The cells in a given column must contain
  information of the same type. For example, if you have a
  ZIP code column, all cells in that column must contain a
  ZIP code, and not some other kind of data. A cell can be
  left blank if a particular column does not apply to that
  record.

- **Calculations:** You can create a *calculated field*, which uses information from another field of the same record and produces a result. For example, if you have a column called "Sales Amount," you could use a formula to create the values in a column called "Sales Commission." (To do so, enter a formula, as explained in Lesson 14.)

 Record Numbering   You might want to add a column that numbers the records. The record number is likely to be the only thing about the record that won't be repeated in another record, and having a unique field could come in handy in advanced databases. Also, if the records are sorted incorrectly, you can use the numbered column to restore the records to their original order.

PLANNING A DATABASE

Before you create your database, you should ask yourself these questions:

- What are the fields that make up an individual record? If you are creating the database to take the place of an existing form (a Rolodex card, information sheet, or address list), use that form to determine which fields you need.

- Which types of data might you want to sort by? If you want to sort by last name, make sure that last name is stored in its own field, and not combined with the first name in a single field. If you want to sort by city, phone number, or ZIP code, make sure that each of these is stored in its own field.

- Which types of data might you want to search for? If you want to search for all contacts who work in a particular sales area, make sure you place sales areas in their own field.

- What is the most often referenced field in the database? (This field should be placed in the first column.)

- What is the longest entry in each column? Use this information to set the column widths. (Or you can make your entries and then use Format Column AutoFit Selection to have Excel adjust the column widths.)

CREATING A DATABASE

To create a database, you don't have to use any special commands. All you do is enter data into the cells as you would enter data on any worksheet. However, as you enter data, you must follow these guidelines:

- Enter field names in the top row of the database. Enter the first record just below this field name's row.

- Type field entries into each cell in a single row to create a record. (You can leave a field blank, but you may run into problems later when you sort the database—that is, if you sort the database by that particular field.)

- Do *not* leave an empty row between the field names and the records or between any records.

- If you want to enter street numbers with the street names at the beginning of the field (such as 155 State Street), start the entry with an apostrophe so that Excel interprets the entry as text instead of as a value. However, note that if you want to enter, for example, One Washington Square Suite 600, you don't need the apostrophe because it begins with text.

- Keep the records on one worksheet. You cannot have a database that spans several worksheets.

 Forget Someone? To add records to a database, either add the rows above the last row in the database (see Lesson 13, "Inserting and Deleting Cells, Rows, and Columns") or select the Data, Form command and enter the additional records using the data form.

USING DATA FORMS TO ADD, EDIT, OR DELETE RECORDS

Data forms are like index cards: there is one data form for each record in the database, as shown in Figure 25.2. You may find it easier to flip through these data form "cards" and edit entries than to edit them as worksheet data. To edit your database using a data form, perform the following steps:

1. Open the Data menu and select Form. You will see a data form that contains the first record in the database (see Figure 25.2.)

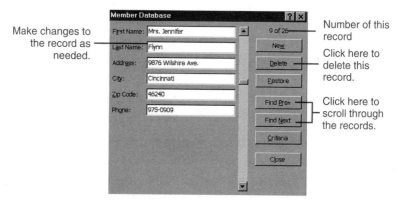

FIGURE 25.2   The data form.

2. The number of the current record appears in the upper-right corner of the form. Flip to the form you want to edit by using the scroll bar, pressing the up or down arrow key, or clicking Find Prev or Find Next.

3. To edit an entry in a record, tab to the text box that contains the entry and type your correction.

4. To delete the current record, click Delete.

5. Repeat steps 2–4 to change as many records as needed.

6. Click the Close button when you're done using the data form.

Come Back! You can restore field data to what it was before you changed it—provided you haven't changed to a different record. To do so, click the Restore button. After you move on to a different record, you'll just have to re-type the field data.

You can also use the data form to add records to the database, as described here:

1. Open the Data menu and choose Form to display the data form.

2. Click the New button.

3. Type an entry into each of the text boxes.

4. Repeat steps 2 and 3 to add additional records.

5. When you finish adding records, click Close.

Template Wizard Use the Template Wizard to create a worksheet template into which you can enter some of the data that you later want to save in a database. For example, you could create a sales worksheet and then link it to a client database so you can save information on the items each client purchases. Just open the Data menu and select Template Wizard. (If you don't see this command, you need to install the Template Wizard add-in.) The Template Wizard walks you step by step through linking cells in the template to fields in a database.

In this lesson, you learned about database basics and how to create a database. In the next lesson, you will learn how to sort the database and find individual records.

26

FINDING AND SORTING DATA IN A DATABASE

In this lesson, you will learn how to sort a database and how to find individual records.

FINDING DATA WITH A DATA FORM

To find records in a database, you use the Criteria Form, in which you tell Excel the specific information or range of information you want to find—the *criteria*. You can look for something specific, such as a person with the last name of Brown, or you can look for a condition that must be evaluated, such as all records containing sales amounts less than $1000. Table 26.1 shows the operators you can use for comparisons.

TABLE 26.1 EXCEL'S COMPARISON OPERATORS

OPERATOR	MEANING
=	Equal to
>	Greater than
<	Less than
>=	Greater than or equal to
<=	Less than or equal to
<>	Not equal to

For example, if you wanted to search for records containing sales amounts greater than $1000, you would enter **>1000** in the Sales field in the criteria form.

When specifying criteria, you can also use the following *wild cards* (characters used to represent information you don't know, or information that is common to many records) when specifying criteria:

?   Represents a single character

*   Represents multiple characters

For example, in the Name field, you could type **M*** to find everyone whose name begins with an M. To find everyone whose three-digit department code has 10 as the last two digits, you could type **?10**.

To find individual records in a database:

1. Open the Data menu and select Form. The Data Form dialog box appears.

2. Click the Criteria button, and the Criteria Form shown in Figure 26.1 appears.

Finds all records with last names that start with L...

...and who live in Indianapolis...

...and whose ZIP code ends in 220

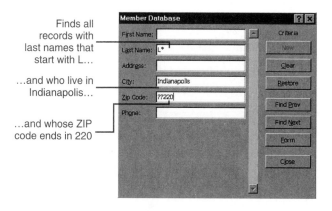

FIGURE 26.1   Selecting search criteria.

3. Type the criteria you would like to use in the appropriate fields. Use only the fields you want to search. For example, if you want to find all Texans whose last name starts with B, type **TX** in the State field, type **B*** in the Last Name field, and leave the other fields blank.

Only Real Data, Please   The data field that you are searching cannot be a calculated field. Excel finds only real (typed in) values.

4. Select Find Next or Find Prev to look through the list of matching records.

5. When you finish reviewing records, click Close.

Sorting Data in a Database

To sort a database, first decide which field to sort by. For example, an address database could be sorted by Name or by City (or it could be sorted by Name within City within State). Each of these sort fields is considered a *key*.

You can use up to three keys when sorting your database. The first key in the above example would be State, the second would be City, and the third would be Name. In other words, all the records would be sorted by state. Then within a state, they would be sorted in order by city. And within each city, the names would be sorted in alphabetical order by name. You can sort your database in ascending or descending order.

Sort Orders   Ascending order sorts records from beginning to end, for example from A to Z or 1 to 100. (Records with a blank sort field appear in front of other records.) Descending order sorts records the opposite way, from Z to A or from 10 to 1.

For the Record   When you select the database range you want to sort, make sure you include all of the *records*, but do not include the column headings (field names). If you select the column heading row, it will be sorted along with all the other rows and may not remain at the top of your database.

Follow these steps to sort your database:

1. Select the area to be sorted. To sort the entire data list, click any cell in the list.

2. Open the Data menu and choose Sort. The Sort dialog box shown in Figure 26.2 appears.

You can enter up to three sorting instructions.

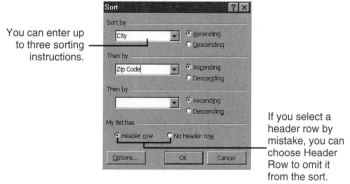

If you select a header row by mistake, you can choose Header Row to omit it from the sort.

FIGURE 26.2   Selecting the sort criteria.

3. Use the Sort By drop-down list to select the first field you want to sort by, and click Ascending or Descending to specify a sort order.

4. To sort by one or two additional fields, select fields from the first and second Then By drop-down lists and choose sort order buttons for each. To remove a sort criteria from a previous sort attempt, open its list box and select (none).

5. Click OK or press Enter.

Undoing a Sort   If the sorting operation does not turn out as planned, you can undo the sort by clicking Undo. To sort even more safely, you might also consider saving a copy of your database file under a different name before sorting. That way, if anything goes wrong, you can open your original database file.

To quickly sort your database by a single field, simply click a cell in that column and click the Sort Ascending or Sort Descending button on the Standard toolbar.

NARROWING YOUR LIST WITH AUTOFILTER

AutoFilter allows you to easily display only a select group of records in your database. For example, you can display the records for only those people who live in Boston. Here's how you use AutoFilter:

1. Click a cell in the database.

2. Open the Data menu, select Filter, and select AutoFilter. Excel displays drop-down list arrow buttons inside each of the heading cells.

3. Click the drop-down arrow for the field you want to use to filter the list. For example, if you want to display records for those people living in Boston, click the City cell's drop-down arrow. A drop-down list appears, as shown in Figure 26.3. This list shows all the entries in the column.

4. Select the entry you want to use to narrow your list. You can use the arrow keys to scroll through the list, or you can type the first character in the entry's name to quickly move to it. Press Enter or click the entry. Excel filters the list so that only the records for people living in Boston appear.

 Undoing a List To return to the full list, open the drop-down list again and choose (All). Or, you can remove the AutoFilter drop-down arrows by selecting Data, Filter, AutoFilter.

Click the arrow to display
the drop-down list.

Select a keyword
to sort by.

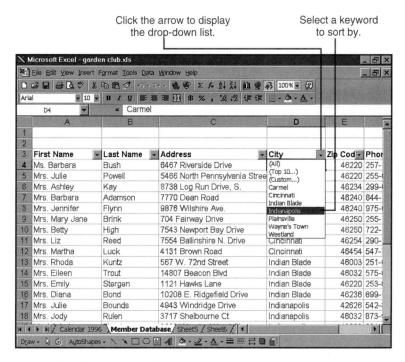

FIGURE 26.3   AutoFilter lets you narrow your list.

The Custom option in the AutoFilter drop-down list lets you apply two criteria values within the current column, or use comparison operators AND and OR. To use the Custom option, click the drop-down list button for the field you want to filter and select Custom. Excel displays the Custom AutoFilter dialog box. Enter your preferences and click OK to filter your data.

The Top 10 option enables you to display all rows that contain the highest or lowest (best or worst) items in a list. For example you could select the top 10 percent (such as the top 10% of sales revenues), or you could select the bottom 10 values in your total list (such as the bottom 10 sales revenues). Choose the Top 10 option in the AutoFilter drop-down list, enter your preferences in the Top 10 AutoFilter dialog box, and then click OK to filter your data.

Look It Up!   With the Lookup Wizard, you can locate one piece of information by looking up something else. For example, if you have a sales database, you could find the name of the salesperson who sold a particular item. To use the Lookup Wizard, open the Tools menu, select Wizard, and select Lookup.

In this lesson, you learned how to find individual records and how to sort and filter your database. In the next lesson, you will learn how to add graphics and other objects to your worksheets.

ADDING GRAPHICS AND OTHER OBJECTS TO WORKSHEETS

27

In this lesson, you will learn how to add graphic objects to your worksheets.

WORKING WITH GRAPHIC OBJECTS

Excel comes with several tools that enable you to add graphic objects to your workbooks and charts. You can add a graphic object created in another program, you can add *clip art* (which is pre-drawn art that comes with Excel and other programs), or you can draw your own graphic objects using the Drawing toolbar.

 Graphic Object A graphic object is anything in your worksheet that isn't data. Graphic objects include things you can draw (such as ovals and rectangles), text boxes, charts, and clip art.

INSERTING CLIP ART

If you have a collection of clip art or pictures that you created and saved using a graphics program or scanner, you can insert those pictures in a worksheet or a chart. To insert a picture, follow these steps:

1. Select the cell in which you want the upper-left corner of the picture placed.

2. Open the Insert menu, choose Picture, and choose
Clip Art. The Microsoft Clip Art Gallery 3.0 dialog box
appears, as shown in Figure 27.1. (You might see a re-
minder that additional clips are stored on the CD-ROM.
Insert the CD and click OK.)

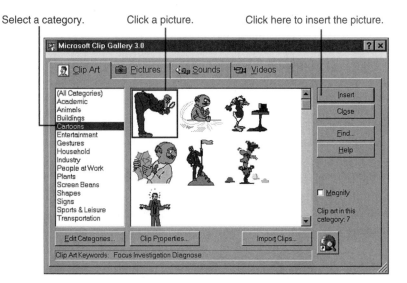

Figure 27.1   You can insert a picture or a clip art file.

3. If necessary, click the Clip Art tab. Then select a category
from the list on the left. For example, click Cartoons.

4. Click an image to select it.

5. Click Insert to insert the image. The image appears in the
worksheet.

You can move the picture by dragging it. To resize the picture,
click on it first to select it, and then drag one of its handles (the
small squares that appear around the image when it's selected).
Drag a corner handle to change both the width and height pro-
portionally. Drag a side handle to change only the width, or drag
a top or bottom handle to change only the height.

INSERTING YOUR OWN CLIP ART, VIDEO CLIPS, OR SOUND CLIPS

Excel 97 allows you to organize your clip art images, sound clips, and video clips in its Clip Gallery. Once you import a file into the Gallery, you can insert it into any Microsoft Office document, including an Excel workbook, Word document, or PowerPoint presentation. Follow these steps to import a file into the Gallery:

1. Open the Insert menu, select Picture, and select Clip Art.

2. Click the tab for the type of file you want to import. For example, to import a video clip, click the Video tab.

3. Click Import Clips.

4. In the file selector dialog box that appears, change to the folder that contains the file you want to import and select the file from the list.

5. Click Open. The dialog box shown in Figure 27.2 appears.

6. Select the category or categories in which you want the clip to appear.

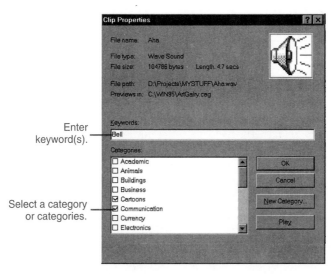

FIGURE 27.2 Select the categories you want to use.

Can't Find an Appropriate Category? You can create a new category if you want, by clicking New Category, entering a name, and clicking OK.

7. In the Keywords text box, enter some keywords that describe the clip. For example, type **Bell**.

8. Click OK, and the clip is added to the Gallery.

To insert the clip into a worksheet, follow the same basic steps that you did to insert clip art: open the Insert menu, select Picture, and select Clip Art. Click the tab for the type of clip you want to insert, and then click the category to which it belongs. Select the clip you want and click Insert to import it into your worksheet.

DRAWING YOUR OWN PICTURES

You can add arrows, text boxes, and other objects to your worksheets or your charts by using the Drawing toolbar. Table 27.1 lists the tools on the Drawing toolbar.

TABLE 27.1   TOOLS ON THE DRAWING TOOLBAR

TOOL	NAME	DESCRIPTION
Draw ▾	Draw	Contains commands for grouping, rotating, and aligning objects
▨	Select Objects	Enables you to select an object
⟳	Free Rotate	Rotates an object
AutoShapes ▾	AutoShapes	Offers tools with which you can create lots of predrawn shapes, such as arrows, stars, and callouts

TOOL	NAME	DESCRIPTION
	Line	Draws a curved or straight line
	Arrow	Draws an arrow
	Rectangle	Draws a square or a rectangle
	Oval	Draws a circle or an oval
	Text Box	Adds text (in a move-able box) to a work-sheet or chart
	Insert WordArt	Adds shaped text
	Fill Color	Changes the color of a selected object
	Line Color	Changes the color of an object's outline
	Font Color	Changes the color of text
	Line Style	Changes the style of a line object
	Dash Style	Changes the default dash style
	Arrow Style	Changes the style of an arrow object
	Shadow	Adds a shadow to an object
	3-D	Makes an object appear 3-D

To use any of the tools on the Drawing toolbar, click the button and drag to create the shape. For example, to create a text box, click the Text Box button. Then click in the worksheet or chart where you want to place the upper-left corner of the text box, and drag downward and to the right to create the text box. Type your message into the box, and then click within the worksheet to deselect the text box.

When you click on a drawn object, handles appear around it to show that it's selected. Once it's selected, you can resize the object by dragging one of its handles outward (to make it bigger) or inward (to make it smaller). You can move an object by dragging it.

 Group Them Together   Excel lets you group objects together so you can move, resize, and format them as a single unit. Press and hold the Shift key and click each object you want to group. Then click the Draw button and select Group.

In this lesson, you learned how to add graphic objects and other objects to your worksheets and charts. You also learned how to use Excel's drawing tools to enhance the appearance of worksheets and charts. Appendix A follows this lesson. If you're new to Windows, you'll find that it's full of helpful information to get you up and running fast.

INDEX